Endorsement

"It's time to get your mind right, and…*Suddenly Wealthy* is going to help you do that. Get reading and then go create some IMPACT in this world!"

~ Todd Durkin, MA, CSCS

"Whether you are a young or experienced professional (athlete), this book will help you adjust and adapt your mentality, lifestyle and overall behaviour and empower you to take control of your life and finances."

~ Athena P. Constantino, The Sports Financial Literacy Academy

"*Suddenly Wealthy* lays out a playbook that is critical for pro athletes who want to be empowered by real-life example and insights that demonstrate how to keep and grow their wealth— well beyond their playing career."

~ Deborah Dubree, Elite Performance Expert and Strategist

"A great athlete can generate an extraordinary income, but…if your outgo exceeds your income, your upkeep will be your downfall. You are here for a long time, not just a good time. *Suddenly Wealthy* delivers powerful wisdom!"

~ Wayne Cotton CLU. CEO Cotton Systems Ltd

"If you are a champion on the court or in the field, you can become a champion with your finances by reading Bonita's book. I highly recommend it."

~ Jim Hayford, Head Men's Basketball Coach, Seattle University

SUDDENLY WEALTHY

AN ATHLETE'S GUIDE TO
WINNING THE MONEY GAME

BONITA K. BELL-ANDERSEN, CLU, CHFC

Published by Vervante, Inc.

Printed in the United States of America
Bonita K. Bell-Andersen, CLU, ChFC
Suddenly Wealthy
ISBN: 978-1-64775-148-7

This book is designed to provide information for professional athletes of all kinds, individuals who receive a large amount of money all at once, or those seeking to learn more about the world of investing principles. There are no guarantees relative to the content within. The understanding is that the publisher and author are not engaged in rendering medical, legal, financial, or other professional services. If professional services or expert assistance is required, the services of a specialist should be sought.

Because of rapid changes in the industry, this book contains information on money management as pertaining to professional athlete statistics as of press time. Therefore, this text should be used only as a general guide and not as the ultimate source of information for this subject.

The purpose of this book is to educate, inspire, motivate, and provide knowledge. The author and Vervante, Inc. shall have neither liability nor responsibility to any person or entity with respect to any loss or damage caused, or alleged to have been caused, directly or indirectly, by the information contained in this book.

This is not an offer of sale of securities. All investing involves risk, and particular investment outcomes are not guaranteed. This book is for informational purposes only and does not constitute an offer to sell, a solicitation to buy, or a recommendation for any security, or an offer to provide advisory, or other services by Bonita K. Bell-Andersen in any jurisdiction in which such offer, solicitation, purchase, or sale would be unlawful under the securities laws of such jurisdiction. Bonita K. Bell-Andersen is an Investment Advisor Representative with a State of Washington Registered Investment Adviser. Advisory services are offered through Freedom Financial Coaching, LLC, a Registered Investment Advisory Firm. Additional information about Bonita K. Bell-Andersen is also available on the SEC's website at www.adviserinfo.sec.gov. Registration with the United States Securities and Exchange Commission or any state securities authority does not imply a certain level of skill or training. Insurance products and services are offered through Independent Agent Bonita Bell-Andersen, an affiliated company. Independent Agent Bonita Bell-Andersen is not affiliated with or endorsed by the Social Security Administration or any government agency.

Acknowledgements

I have learned firsthand how much of a "team effort" writing a book can be! This book came about because of a variety of "synchronistic" occurrences. What does it mean to have synchronicity?[1] Carl Jung first introduced it, saying that events are "meaningful coincidences" if they occur with no causal relationship yet seem to be meaningfully related." This really began for me when Robin Colucci reached out, asking if I needed help in writing a book.[2] Because of the unusual circumstances, I felt like I better get going or I might be struck by lightning or something!

That began a multi-year endeavor, which has happily culminated in the creation of this book. Since I am not a professional athlete, some wondered why in the world I was doing this. The answer was that I continually felt called to get this done, bring this perspective to the market, share my own learnings and experiences from my life, and in the end it was Treya Klassen of DeHoCo[3] who poured her heart and soul into training our independent investment advisors, that gave me my final answer.

Someone had said that athletes would never listen to me—Treya said, "Really, why not you?" Why not me indeed!

To my husband, Butch, who has been eternally patient throughout the process of writing this book, to my children, Jennifer, Angie, and Rachel and their spouses and ten children, and Butch's children, Darren, Troy, Justin, and Brett, and their spouses and twelve children (yes, that is 22 grandchildren!), and all the extended family, I thank you for your encouragement and unending curiosity in the progress of this project. It could also not have happened without the editing skills of Dawn Mena, and the web development skills of Matt Dragos.

To those in the investment world who opened my eyes to the academically structured way of investing, all the wonderfully supportive back office cheerleaders who make it happen every day, and my fellow financial advisors in the industry, thank you for your love and encouragement—it means the world to me!

But most of all, my eternal thanks goes to Robin Colucci, who reached out wondering if I needed help in writing a book, and then nurtured me and patiently coached me all the way to the end. Thank you, Robin, for your expert book-writing assistance!

Dedication

This book is dedicated to all those who have big financial surprises happen in their life (the good, the bad and the ugly) and are willing to listen and be coached as to how to handle it for the best outcome. I am also dedicating it to my family, near and far, who always modeled, and taught me the value of, hard work and always pushing on and through the challenges of life.

And to my dear friends (you know who you are)—thanks for always believing in me and encouraging me to push on through thick and thin. *Suddenly Wealthy* has been a labor of love, and through it all I have prayed for inspiration and direction on how to proceed. My prayer is that all who read this book will feel that inspiration to then implement these principles into their financial life. As Yoda said, "Do. Or do not. There is no try."[4]

Table of Contents

Part 1:
The Advantages and Pitfalls of Sudden Wealth

Part 2:
Keep and Grow Your Money

Foreword

When I found out that Bonita Bell-Andersen (I know her as Bonnie) was writing a book, I was thrilled, because hers is a voice that is deeply needed in our times. She is not your typical financial advisor, or even the typical business type that deals with athletes, and when I think of my own book, *Get Your Mind Right*, I also think of how crucial it is to get your mind right around your finances.

We are faced with many possible forms of financial crisis and those crisis tentacles can penetrate deeply into all aspects of life, and especially that of athletes who are young and are given a bucketload of money at a very early age. The decisions we make today may in fact dictate how things will go for us for the rest of our lives. It is imperative that all of us be aware of the financial issues and decisions that Bonnie brings to light, and take action to protect and grow our wealth for decades to come.

I am a champion of creating crucial aspects of success—whether that be in business, sports, health, or relationships, and getting your mind right with your finances is a bedrock component of this. Getting your mind right around money doesn't happen as easily as flipping a light switch—you need to start with repeating a mantra that I often share with the professional athletes I train: "*Control the controllables and stop worrying about things you can't change.*"

What DO you control? Your waking hours, your interactions with others, how you spend your time, and who you spend your time with, what you listen to, what you watch, what you eat, how much you exercise, and a million other things! The point is to create the life you want to live—don't let two, three, five years go by without getting things set up financially so that you are then taken care of financially hopefully for the rest of your life!

Start with dreaming big—think about what it would look like to have your finances handled for the rest of your life. All the goals that I go for, and I like to call the BIG ones "BHAG's" (big, hairy, audacious goals), should be the basis on which you start crafting that amazing future, with your finances all handled. And here's something to consider—maybe in order to do that, you might have to give up some immediate desires, some of the things you "think" you should have right NOW in order to start laying down the foundation of what could be an amazing future.

All of this "crafting the future" stuff is going to start with how you think about finances, and your thoughts are ultimately going to determine your legacy. Bonnie talks a lot about this in the chapter on developing your mindset, and I have a caution here. Take a look at the mistakes other athletes have made, benefit from what they say they have learned, and incorporate those lessons now so that you never make them. A great way to get yourself pointed in the right direction is to start every day with a focused morning ritual where you decide how your day is going to go—you can do this with some morning meditation, prayer, reading inspirational books, and even reading parts of this book to remind yourself of the financial principles that you are incorporating into your life. Everything counts. Everything begins with the way you think because your thoughts become your words, your words become your flesh, your flesh becomes your actions, your actions become your habits, your habits become your character, and your character ultimately becomes your legacy.

You may be saying, "But Todd, I know that I am going to face trials and obstacles that are going to be really tough to overcome." I know that! What I've found is that mental toughness, spiritual fortitude, and an indomitable spirit will keep you moving forward towards the successful financial future that you are envisioning. Stay the course. Stop and think about every financial decision you make every day—ask yourself if that decision is moving you towards your financial BHAG or not! When you press forward, your life tends to be changed forever for the better because you know that no matter what, you are focusing on the principles and practices that will win the day in the end. And that is entirely what getting your mind right is all about!

Habits will make or break you. What are your rules? What are your best practices—are you asking yourself good questions on the financial choices you can make, and whether or not they will serve you long term? Design your rules so that they support your good habits. It's critical that you set strong winning habits that will create a championship mindset in you. Those strong winning habits will foster strong routines in your life, especially your financial life, and this will help you manifest high-octane fuel to turbocharge your results. Everyone around you will know that you have a no-nonsense approach to winning the financial game, and they better not mess with you!

A thought about coaching—I love coaching, and it is my life—I've always sought out good coaching for myself personally as well as professionally. One of the reasons I believe in coaching so much is because I believe in the "growth mindset" and have a continual thirst for learning. Realize that you need a financial coach, or investor coach, who will keep you on track, talk you off the ledge when you want to do something that will damage you financially, and will hold you accountable and remind you of your ultimate goals you are going for. Bonnie is one of those investor coaches and here is what you look for in an investor coach:

1. **An investor coach cares.** I love this saying, "People don't care how much you know until they know how much you care."

2. **An investor coach listens.** I know that she has had to train herself to listen twice as much as she speaks. My experience with a great coach is that when they open their mouth, their intent is for their speech to be full of wisdom and experience.

3. **An investor coach holds you accountable.** Not only do great coaches provide guidelines, show you the correct exercises, and give you a list of items to work on, but they hold you accountable for your actions.

4. **An investor coach motivates you.** Great coaches usually know where to find the right buttons to push—she is going to try her hardest to do exactly that!

5. **An investor coach is growth-minded.** This author has never rested on her laurels, so to speak. She also continues to grow and learn.

6. **An investor coach has a champion's mindset.** Winning begets winning, just as losing begets losing—this investor coach is a winner and will help you stay on the path that leads to your ultimate success, whatever that might be!

7. **An investor coach loves helping people.** Great coaches have a strong sense of purpose and mission—it's their calling. That's why they love helping people. I can tell you for sure that writing this book, and the crazy things that have happened along the way for her, has helped her realize that this book is really important, and that it will help a LOT of people.

There's no reason why you can't have an extraordinary life. Establish good habits, rules to follow, best practices—and then maniacally follow them. Remember that all the temptations, all the crazy business opportunities that will come your way, all the obstacles, or challenges, or family or friend situations in life that seem daunting or too big, remember that it is an opportunity to get stronger and better. You are always stronger and better than you think!

It's time to get your mind right, and it all starts NOW. I have a saying that states, "Live a life worth telling a story about... what's your story?" NOW is the time to craft up the most amazing story you can imagine. *Suddenly Wealthy* is going to help you do that. It's time for ACTION. Get reading and then go create some IMPACT in this world!

Todd Durkin, MA, CSCS
Founder, Fitness Quest 10 & Todd Durkin Enterprises
Author, Get Your Mind Right; WOW Book; The IMPACT Body Plan
Under Armour, Member of Performance Training Team
Podcaster, The Todd Durkin IMPACT Show

Introduction

"Money talks" (meaning that money has influence) is an old financial saying, cited in print in various forms all the way back to the 1700s. "Money talks, wealth whispers" is a modern variation that was explained by Dorothy Donegan, a veteran jazz pianist, in 1989: *"Money talks but wealth whispers . . . If you got a lot of money you don't need to talk about it, it speaks quietly for itself. If you don't have real money, you're just talking loud and drawing a crowd."*

If you are meeting me for the first time, a few words of introduction will help you see where I am coming from with this book. I have come a long way in my life, learned many lessons (some the hard way, some very expensive as well). I was pretty much self-taught in financial matters—growing up I did not get much direction from my parents, wonderful as they were! I have made LOTS of mistakes along the way. Twenty years ago, a tremendously difficult marriage breakup caused an entire left turn in my life, forcing me to reinvent who I was and what I was going to do moving forward. It was at that point I went into the financial services industry.

As I researched for this book, I saw example after example of athletes who are great at their craft, but the extraordinary money handed to them many times would turn their life into a train wreck. Over time as I gained years of experience with the investment industry, broker dealers, and the like, I began searching for a better way to be an advisor with the end client being the focus instead of the focus being on products or commissions. I knew I needed to find something that I had confidence in because, after all, I was then turning around and advising clients about how I suggested they move forward! I became very passionate about this whole process, and decided to write a book that encapsulated all the lessons I've learned, the importance of coaching, and the successes I've had in my own life as well as the experiences with clients by working with the methods detailed in this book.

Money doesn't change you, it just makes you "more" of who you already are.[5] The strategies, training and education contained in this book are designed to empower you to have breakthroughs in your thinking and behavior with regard to money and investing.[6] I know I've made a ton of mistakes in my own life with money, and having gotten my financial education the hard way, that's why I am passionate about sharing these nuggets of wisdom with you. With these tools in hand, you have the potential to effectively make proactive decisions about how you can get on track to achieve, and even sustain, your American Dream and what you want to accomplish in your life. The problem I see is that there is a lot of financial advice out there for athletes, as well as a lot of financial disasters. As I researched the issues around people receiving a lot of money very quickly, I realized that not only do I have something to say about making mistakes with money, I also know that the systems and processes I have in my hands are perfect for helping athletes transform their relationship with money. I know that I can bring a new perspective to this, especially after an arrogant LA-based advisor told me, to my face, that athletes would never listen to an older, white female.

The fundamental premise upon which I've written this book is this: You as an athlete can be successful with your financial windfalls, can sidestep the financial landmines, and can set yourself up for a lifetime of financial success. I will show you what I perceive to be the realities of the investment world, what to watch out for, and especially how to craft the life you'd like to live. This is so significant because the cards are stacked against you—in many cases you are fairly young, have not had a long history of managing money, can be impetuous or preyed upon by bad apples, and can benefit from guidance and coaching in the world of financial management and long term success. Just like you have coaches for your preferred sport, I will take you step by step through the methodology and why it works.

My goal is that by reading this book you will gain some clarity and confidence. Clarity on what to do to manage your newfound wealth and the confidence to do it.

Here's the best way to approach the book so that you get the most value. Read it in its entirety, then go back and reread it, executing the steps the second time through. Use the worksheets to guide you and discover what you need to do, what actions you need to take, and the future you dream of creating. Realize that you can contact me for further clarification for your own personal situation at bookachatwithbonita.com. My goal is to help you utilize this methodology for the best outcome.

As an advisor and investor coach, I have used and taught these ideas and concepts to all of my clients over the years. I encourage you to visit **www.suddenlywealthy.net**, our website, for a complimentary download designed to deepen your understanding of what is being taught herein. The steps in this book are designed to help you focus on what is important in keeping your wealth now that you have made it. Tiny movements in your thoughts and actions will build and build, creating a wonderful legacy for you over time. All great contests come down to the final seconds, the last step over the finish line, and in this case, all the dollars along the way, up to the final dollar that cements your legacy, and helps you create a life and legacy that is truly the stuff of champions.

PART 1

The Advantages and Pitfalls of Sudden Wealth

"You only live once, but if you do it right, once is enough."

~ Mae West

1

So, You Just Got Rich: The Unique Challenges

Maybe the day you became "wealthy" started out like any other day, and you were caught by surprise when you won the pro-athlete lottery and got the ultimate offer, the multi-7-figure contract,[7] or maybe it's joining your first pro team and getting paid more than you've ever earned before. In that initial moment when you realize you stepped into sudden wealth, perhaps a wave of relief and euphoria washes over you. It might feel, for a moment at least, that all your cares are behind you and you'll never have to worry about money again.[8]

Watching any athlete play their first pro game, I'm struck by the hours of practice, sacrifice, and devotion it took to get there. All of the blood, sweat, and tears that went in to put *you* among the elite of the elites in your sport shows your capacity to accomplish much in your life.[9] This is considering that only two or three players out of every 10,000 in the major men's sports in the U.S. (namely football, basketball, baseball, and hockey) will go on from high school, to college, and then to pro sports.[10] The statistics for women athletes are pretty much the same, not many get to experience the pro level.

Maybe it surprised you when that initial shot of euphoria was followed by a nagging anxiety. When you realized that just as fast as you got this money, you could lose it. Your fears likely were confirmed when you noticed how people started to treat you differently, that they came at you with new expectations, and lots of ideas for where you could "invest" your newfound wealth. Discipline in finance means you make rules for yourself and how you handle your money and stick with them. You decide what percent of your income you're going to save each month, and you decide how much of your fortune you're willing to allocate to help friends and family or to spend on vacations. Even on a relatively small contract, you can still live prudently and comfortably, be wise, and plan for the future, all while having fun now!

Attaining wealth is one thing. The challenge of keeping it is another. Here is how you RUIN this whole thing and quickly get into trouble: Immediately buy all the things you think you want but can easily live without. Get an expensive new home (or two), exotic cars, planes, yachts, luxury goods, jewelry, collectibles and other toys—it adds up quickly! Never mind remembering that many things require ongoing fees, maintenance, taxes, insurance, or even a staff of people to keep them up. Most people don't go belly up for buying one or two things but going nuts with endless buying binges can even break billionaires these days. It is important to avoid the temptation to become an instant high-roller or to live too large. If you are jumping into real estate, think about the maintenance, upkeep, and overall care of any of those properties, including the paying of taxes!

Many suddenly wealthy pro athletes have ended up broke because of external pressures from friends and family who show up at the door with their hands out or looking to the athlete to "invest" in a new business idea. There is no shortage of examples of pro athlete players blowing all their cash almost as soon as they get it and then being left with nothing to show for their careers but a long list of injuries and a mountain of debt. Poor decisions can be tied to a feeling of entitlement, that feeling of, "I've worked really hard, so I deserve to spend as much as I want," or "I have this, so I need that," or the ever-present FOMO (fear of missing out) complex, "Everyone else is doing it, why shouldn't I?" Don't allow yourself to get pulled into rationalizing an expensive lifestyle as being important to "who you are." Decide now that who you are is an athlete in a new kind of sport. The sport of financial freedom. If you dedicate even a fraction of the commitment to financial mastery and long-term wealth that you have into your sport, you should be set for life, and have plenty to hand down to your charities and heirs. The best thing you can do now is to acknowledge that one day your pro career will end, and you will still have a long life to live. Prepare now for when your run as a pro is over and the paychecks wind down. Take this rare opportunity to do everything you can to make sure you're set for life. It's fine to have fun, but as every champion knows, you've got to keep your head in the game. When you score big during a game, you celebrate, but you don't stop to pop a champagne bottle. You still need to get back to business and play the rest of the game.

Have some fun, celebrate your newfound wealth, but remember that the financial success game is a long one. One big score at the beginning will never guarantee a win. In my research for this book, I saw time and again stories of young, highly-paid athletes who've run up huge debts, and are wondering how this could happen. If you have fallen prey to financial issues, don't beat yourself up because you "let" this happen. Just recognize that it's time to take charge of your finances, and understand that in the game of money, what determines the winners isn't how much you earn, but how much you keep.

Despite the perception that a shortage of money is the root of all problems, when you acquire wealth you will quickly discover that this is simply not true. Becoming wealthy doesn't mean you'll never have to worry about money again. To the contrary, it means you'll need to up-level your sense of personal responsibility. Problems still exist, and money often magnifies them.

Obtaining money suddenly can catch you off guard. According to CNBC, lottery winners are more likely to go bankrupt within three to five years than the average American. "Studies found that instead of getting people out of financial trouble, winning the lottery got people into more trouble, since bankruptcy rates soared for lottery winners three to five years after winning."[11] Coming back to sports, according to *Sports Illustrated*, 78% of NFL players file for bankruptcy just two years after retirement. Five years after retirement, 60% of NBA players suffer the same fate. According to a study in the National Bureau of Economic Research (NBER), close to 16% of the NFL players in the study who were drafted between 1996—2003 filed for bankruptcy within 12 years of retirement.[12]

If you're like a lot of suddenly wealthy folks, all those years you fantasized about having money, you didn't think much beyond paying off all your debts or buying your dream home or car. And now, with loads of cash and no clear plan for what to do with it, you suddenly feel extraordinarily vulnerable and unsure of where to turn or whom you can trust. If that thought makes you anxious, Bingo! You're thinking accurately.

Don't fight it, and don't push it down. Rest assured that your anxiety is real and NOT to be ignored. In fact, it's your friend. It's that part of you that recognizes the need to step up your game and learn to master a new arena (or playing field). Fact is, until you educate yourself and put a plan in place to protect and grow your wealth, you *should* be feeling anxious.[13] As an athlete investor, try as you might, sometimes you might find it difficult to overcome your own human tendencies. If my guess is right, you are probably a pretty intense individual. You may think that you can make investment decisions based on logic, but typically emotions such as trust, loyalty, hope, greed, and fear can get in the way and drive your investing decisions.

Realize that if you allow financial chaos to begin, you are going to get financial chaos in the end. Start disciplining yourself right now about your finances, just like you discipline yourself to go to the gym in the off season. Let's get started on a more positive future.

Here's why, when you're suddenly wealthy, chances are you have one or more of the following circumstances working against you:

Less Room for Trial and Error

I recently saw a joke that NFL stands for "not for long."[14] Joking aside, this is a real concern for all pro athletes or anyone who gains great wealth in a short period of time. The slow wealth-builders have had a chance to refine their spending habits and to develop their investing skills using smaller sums (with less at stake) over several years. The suddenly wealthy may not have the same luxury of learning gradually by trial and error, and the impact of one bad decision could cost not just thousands, but millions. It's not just your imagination that this all might seem overwhelming; there are forces out to get you — or at least your money. Being prepared will help you counter the very real forces out there that want you to spend, spend, spend. What better way to step out into the world after your athletic career is over than with your finances under control? It's easy to think there's plenty of time to worry about money later, once your time is freed up and you are looking forward to getting established with other endeavors. But the truth is, it's never too early for good habits.

A Shortage of Role Models

Families with old money tend to have a solid infrastructure of long-term assets and elders who model behaviors that keep wealth in the family. Many professional athletes grow up in circumstances ranging from extreme poverty to middle-class. Once you begin to earn, your income can shoot up into income numbers that are 1,000 times more than your parents earned in a lifetime. Entering here can be dangerous ground, because most people who grow up in lower-income environments have no role models for generating and growing wealth. This leaves a lot of athletes vulnerable to all kinds of pitfalls that could cause you to lose your wealth, from predatory con-artists, to big dream investment schemes, and even your own generosity.

Being Visible and Vulnerable, Especially Around the Entourage

Like the old song says, nobody knows you when you're down and out, but once word gets out that you have acquired a pro contract, the entourage manifests around you like a cloud. Suddenly, a lot of so-called friends, as well as your family, are milling around. The parties never seem to stop and you are expected to pick up the tab (without looking at the bill). And your team? It would be natural to be nervous because you are new, and you want to make a good impression on your new teammates. But if you make over-spending a new standard, before you know it there is a big fat hole in your newfound wealth.

If suddenly there is a bunch of people hanging around, then think about why they are there. This matters because if you want to hang on to your wealth, you've got to develop some of the habits that help you keep and grow your wealth. You haven't had time to practice, and you've got to master them quickly.

Don't put this out on Facebook—keep it to yourself! Did anyone tell you to keep it a secret that you just became rich? It's a smart thing to do, you don't want to become a target. You are possibly going to have to think about remaining protected from your friends and family, as old acquaintances may even suddenly be calling you. You can become a great money manager, and a role model for your buddies. If you develop a philosophy of "big pockets and short fingers" (you're not an easy touch who is liberal with your money at the drop of a hat), this can serve you well and be a lesson for countless pro athletes who believe that "spend now and worry about it later" is the right way to live.

Your family and friends may ask you for help or to partic-
ipate in financial dealings you don't, or shouldn't, be involved
with. Other friends or family may become envious or treat you
differently. They may come to you and ask for money, and you
COULD say no, but at what cost? Don't feel like you have to set
up the Bank of Family & Friends, and don't feel like you need
to buy everything for everyone. It is important to protect your
assets, you haven't even figured out yet how to set up a budget.

Then there is the worst of the lot: scam artists or criminals
who go after you. Maybe you've heard of kidnap and ransom
insurance before (yes, it's real). Sudden wealth is visible wealth,
so it can attract predators. Often, people receiving this good fortune are featured in the news.[15] This can especially happen to pro
athletes, whose salaries are broadcast through reporting on the
draft, or trades, or the outcome of contract negotiations.

Determine to what degree you will help family and friends,
and what your limits are. Set unbreakable rules around this. Be
cautious about committing to ongoing financial obligations.
Instead of handing out money, think of ways to invest in the person you seek to help, such as funding their college education. It is
also important to know that how you give money to people may
create tax events for them — or for you. The parents of a newly
minted pro athlete might say, "We raised you—we took care of
you—you need to take care of us now." Of course, you want to
help! The friend might say, "We always looked out for you." This
could be traumatizing or cause a guilt trip. OF COURSE, you
want to honor your parents, and the first thing many have done
is buy their Mama a house. But after a while, when the requests
keep coming and never stop, the constant "favors," requests, pleas,
and sometimes even demands can be wearing. The question is:
"Do you learn from it? Do you have a strategy for dealing with
it? Or do you keep giving in to the demands and the requests?"[16]

You've got your family, your friends, your teammates—then
you have your really personal relationships, the kind of relationships that make babies. Do they love you, or is it your money
they love? This is the big one that shows up almost immedi-

ately. Does he/she really find you fascinating, or just your bank balance? Are they really won over by your wit or experience, or does he/she just hope to bleed you dry? The term "gold-digger" comes to mind here—a person who dates others purely to extract money from them. The stereotype is a woman who strives to marry a wealthy man, but it could totally be the other way around! In speaking about family in particular, either significant others or spouses, a related subject is how you choose to bring children into the world. This can complicate things in a hurry. One thing few young athletes ever anticipate is fathering multiple children and paying child support and alimony to multiple ex-wives. What's even worse is that once they retire, some have put the divorce rate as high as 85% among NFL, NBA, MLB, and even National Hockey League players.[17] One agent even thought that there were more kids conceived out of wedlock than there are players in the NBA. You don't want to be the guy arrested for nonpayment of child support, which carries mandatory jail time. As with your financial matters, be wise in the personal relationships you develop along the way. It can be tricky, but if you really get to know people first, then hopefully some of these personal challenges can be avoided.

A Barrage of Business Opportunities

Predators aren't the only people to watch out for. Visible wealth can also attract con artists, criminals, and long lost "friends" who show up at your door with their hand out. Unfortunately, the most dangerous predators blend in. They're not obviously deranged, and while they're morally deviant, they are skilled at hiding it. These predators have a callous disregard for the rights of others. They charm and manipulate for their own gain, with no sense of guilt or regret. They look for opportunities to get close and will exploit those opportunities when the time is right. These unscrupulous individuals may seek money for fraudulent investments, while others may engage in underhanded business practices. I've even heard many examples of immediate family members taking advantage of a professional athlete's contract to secure loans or make investments on the player's behalf without the player's knowledge.

Let's say that a buddy calls you with a business opportunity—will you tell him that your "advisor" will look at it? NO! Right now, you need to realize that your most important asset is YOU. You need to educate yourself about those business opportunities and what is right for you—and that doesn't happen overnight. So the question will be, "How am I going to get good information if I don't know who to trust?" In the beginning, you will often be guided by your teammates or your agent to check this or that out. Ultimately, though, you will need to determine the areas that are right for you, your long-term goals, and who you feel is trustworthy.[18]

If you are a religious person, then you may be familiar with Matthew 7:16 which says, "Ye shall know them by their fruits." This is referring to a proper test of someone's character. The analogy here is that people do not judge a tree by its leaves, or bark, or flowers. What is important is the fruit which it bears. The flowers may be beautiful, the foliage thick and green; but it is the "fruit" that we can eat, that can nourish us, and help us grow strong. The person approaching you with a business opportunity may seem fair, but the "conduct"—the fruit—is to determine if there is danger for you. Ask yourself if you know anything about the industry that this opportunity is in. Do they want you to understand what you are getting into, or does it seem like they are rushing you to a decision?

Just because someone is honest doesn't mean that their business idea is a good one (or good for YOU). If you didn't get rich by your own efforts in business (like self-made millionaires), chances are high that you should avoid becoming everyone's business backer. If you knew nothing about venture capital and private equity last week, getting a big check today is not likely at all to change your knowledge any time soon. If anyone, even someone you trust, approaches you with a business opportunity, think twice about getting involved until you have a thorough understanding of what you are getting into. Vet all opportunities. Carefully screen and investigate before you write any checks or sign any papers. Don't take just any one person's word for it. Get the support you need by finding trusted mentors and gaining new knowledge and skills.

So how in the world do you protect yourself? Be careful of promises, flattery, fast talk, gifts, or anything that might be an attempt to deflect your attention from an intended manipulation. If an investing opportunity seems too good to be true, it probably is, and the person who brings it to you may be at worst, dishonest, at best, naive. Make reasonable inquiries about anyone who wishes to get close to you. Become aware of what you think your weak spots might be, and be aware of what blind spots you may have. Your best defense will be a great offense. Ask yourself what is the worst thing that could happen—could it bankrupt you? Will you be asked to pay the bills if the venture goes under?

There will be those that try to manipulate you to what they want you to do. Be careful of who you trust. Ask lots of questions and understand what you are doing before investing in anything. If you sense that something is not right with a person's behavior, it may save you a lot of grief! Especially listen to yourself if you feel like something is amiss.[19] As Steve Jobs said in his address to graduating students at Stanford University, "Don't let the noise of others' opinions drown out your own inner voice. And most important, have the courage to follow your heart and intuition."

Nervous?

If thinking about all this has you feeling even more anxious, this is a good thing because now that you are aware of the dangers, you can find some relief by focusing on the principles that will help put you on the right track, so you can take care of yourself (and your wealth) now and far into the future. Here are some steps to get you started.

- **Educate Yourself:** Success leaves clues. Study what the long-term wealthy do. To learn which investments are the best fit for you requires some degree of trial and error. By no means will every investment you make pay off. Investing always carries the possibility of losing money, but the lessons don't have to be as severe or painful when you educate yourself first.

- **Create a Structure for Wealth:** You already understand structure and discipline to some extent, or you wouldn't have gotten this far as an athlete. You've already spent hours practicing and training, reviewing film of your own performance to work on your weaknesses, watching your diet, working weekends and holidays, and the like. Know that you can apply that same discipline and put in place a structure for keeping and building your wealth. When it comes right down to it, a successful structure for wealth will always involve saving, smart investing, and being mindful in making financial decisions.

- **Learn How to Be a Successful Investor:** Now that you have this money, you have the opportunity to grow into the type of person who knows what to do with it, how to handle it, and use this windfall to the max. Like anyone else, you will encounter challenges, obstacles and less than perfect conditions. But with every step you take, you will grow stronger, more confident, and more skilled, even if you feel like you could do better in some areas. If you experience a financial setback, then see it as a challenge, learn from it, and move on. But don't give up on your long-term vision. Taking even the most basic steps will get you in the game and in touch with what is most important. Even slow progress is better than none at all, especially now when you're young. Set yourself up and position yourself for lasting financial success without regret.[20]

You should only have to *become* rich once. Your career, or your moment in the limelight, will seem to go by in a flash. After that, you will have the rest of your life to live. The decisions you make today will determine whether you continue to build on the wealth you've acquired or if you'll have to start over.[21] If you are lucky enough to be a rookie that gets picked in the first round draft with a huge contract attached, by all means have some fun, AND save a lot for the future.

What You Can Learn from the "Average" Millionaire

"Someone is sitting in the shade today because
someone planted a tree a long time ago."

~ Warren Buffett

You might be surprised to know that 88% of millionaires in this country are first-generation affluent.[22] However, the average millionaire is more likely to die rich than the suddenly wealthy. This is not new information, as according to the traits of millionaires described in *The Millionaire Next Door*, by Thomas J. Stanley and William D. Danko,[23] 70% of the suddenly wealthy lose it all within a year and the biggest reason is that they had no idea what to do with their newfound wealth.[24] Good news is you can learn some great strategies from the slow wealth builders and adapt them to your situation. One strategy you'll find consistently, and as much in millionaires today as ones from the 20th century, is that they live not just within their means, they live below it. Way below.

Live on a Little, Earn a Lot: Those that have built a fortune over time live on only a small portion of their wealth. The median millionaire spends $90,000 a year while earning $250,000 in annual income pre-tax, an impressive 64% savings rate.[25] They are focused on saving and investing, not spending. The millionaire next door has wealth but doesn't show it. They live well below their means, thus their wealth is less visible to their neighbors. These folks drive a modest, usually older car, and still live in a house they bought years ago. Contrast that with the pressures you may face. You've heard of keeping up with the Joneses? Your problem is that you won't be trying to keep up with the folks from your old neighborhood. You'll be hanging out with the veterans on your team, so for you, keeping up with the "Joneses" will look more like keeping up with the Wilson's[26] or Brady's[27] or Federer's[28] or Ronaldo's.

Allow yourself to indulge, but maybe take the hint about not being too visible and avoid over-the-top spending that extends you far beyond your means. Avoid oversharing. Be private with what is going on in your financial world. Most players come into professional sports unequipped to handle the temptations brought on by the sudden windfall that a big contract brings. Many give in to enticements like cars, houses, fancy clothes, jewelry, gambling, and "exciting" business opportunities.

The other side of the coin is the pressures—the pressure to fit in at your new club, the pressure to look like you know what you are doing, the pressure to just follow what the other members of your team are saying you need to do, and just do it! This can be heady stuff, and my problem is I can't MAKE you want to get educated about your finances. While you may have the urge to spend like the gravy train is never going to end, the best thing you can do is prepare now for when your run as a pro is over, and the paychecks wind down. As Olympian Gold Medalist Lauryn Williams told me when we met in Scottsdale, AZ in 2017, "My advice to athletes: make a plan. Don't spend a dollar until you know where it's going. Every dollar has a job."[29]

As the following story illustrates, sometimes you as a young athlete may not take advice well. You would hope that most agents, and especially your teammates, would give you good advice. Sometimes, however, when things go wrong, the guy you blame the most could be you. You definitely have come into this with your own ideas and your own mind, and you'd probably say that you've always been that way. When you first walk into that pro athlete locker room, you want to fit in, you want to be like your teammates. For the most part, this desire to fit in could be what gets you into trouble. Quietly moving into this new reality may be difficult. For example, if you've been driving a perfectly good older Honda one day, and then you get drafted, the following might happen.

In 2017, retired MLB athlete Brian Barton[30] and I were attending a sports financial advisor conference. Brian is a great guy, very down to earth and easy going, yet tells it like it is. He experienced a lot of pressure from teammates to get rid of his current car and buy a very expensive "upgrade," just because "he could." As Brian says, "It's hard to prepare. You don't know what's being thrown at you. Your strongest gift could be growing up broke. Don't change your lifestyle right away. Get comfortable with saying NO."

Think of Wealth as a Tool: Millionaires do not consider wealth as cash on hand to spend freely. They think of it as a tool, a resource, to get what they want in life. Amassing money isn't the goal. Happiness is the goal. Doing the things that make life meaningful—maybe travel, reading, writing, spending time with friends, it could be a thousand things — is the goal. Money is useful because it can help you do these things.[31] It buys time, it helps you meet your goals, it makes life easier. Whatever the size or shape of the ball is in your sport, remember that it is just a tool to help you play the game. Money is no different!

Set Aside Money for Taxes: Millionaires take into account that higher income means higher taxes and make sure to set aside enough to cover the tax bill when Uncle Sam comes knocking every year. Be wise, avoid debt, optimize the automatic tax withholding from your contract, set up a budget for yourself, and really think about what you need to set aside, beginning with taxes, before you spend anything.

Save 20 Percent of Net Income or More: Even after taxes, most millionaires sock away a significant portion of their net income. Many who take this path accumulate wealth over time by investing nearly 20 percent of their take-home income each year.[32] For most millionaires, this requires enormous financial discipline and long-term commitment. An athlete's situation can vary from a minimal salary that's not much different than entry level in any professional career to massive wealth in the tens of millions.

Pandemics and Other Unforeseen Problems

With the advent of the COVID-19 pandemic in 2020, several situations developed with players taking pay cuts as well as coaches.[33] The bottom line was that many leagues were trying to hold the line while letting a wide number of dynamics play out. With all the challenges for vendors that take care of games played in large stadiums with thousands of fans in attendance, no one is quite sure how the future is going to look. Time will tell how this all settles out. In the meantime, the following are the statistics on how much players, both male and female, have made up to this point.

Here's some interesting statistics on average player salaries for male-dominated sports:

Major League Soccer: The average MLS player earned $411,926 in guaranteed compensation in 2018, according to the MLS players' union, but the median (a specific point in the full spectrum of salaries both high and low)[34] was $179,000, indicating that outsized compensation for a few players pulled that average up.[35] A full third of the league, 238 players, earned less than $100,000.

National Football League: The median salary (that point right in the middle) for all NFL players is $860,000.[36] For perspective, a starting one-year contracted rookie in the NFL has a minimum income of $435,000. Most of the attention from the press is on the stunningly high incomes of top quarterbacks, sometimes receiving upward of $25 to $30 million or more per year. The average salary for all quarterbacks is $5,766,000, but the median income is $1,100,000.

Major League Baseball: As one of the biggest sports leagues in America with TV viewers reaching into the millions, Major

League Baseball can afford to pay its players handsomely. The *average* salary for a player in the MLB stood at $4.36 million in 2019.[37] However, MLB's median salary, the level an equal number earn above and below, dropped from $1.65 million to $1.5 million, still a pretty good paycheck!

National Basketball Association: The *average* NBA player salary is $7.7 million for the season.[38] That number is up from an average salary of almost $6.4 million for the previous season, according to Basketball Reference.

The range of what your income could be varies wildly—no telling what the cards may hold for you.

Female Athletes' Earnings

The gender pay gap crosses industries, so it is not a surprise that women in sports also get short-changed. Female athletes have publicized and protested the issue of pay disparities for decades. Women behind the scenes also earn less (meaning those in the marketing department, as well as a myriad of other support activities). The battle for equal pay in sports started with the Women's Tennis Association in the 1970s when a group of female athletes started their own women-only tennis circuit to protest male tournament winners getting higher pay.[39]

One of the most successful efforts toward female athletes receiving equitable pay discrepancy is being led by an organization called the SheIS Collective. It launched to the public in May 2018 and made history by becoming the first organization to bring together leagues, organizations, athletes, and business leaders from across the men's and women's sports world in support of one mission—to connect with and mobilize fans to grow women's sports. It is working to ensure that women can pursue careers as athletes without going broke by creating a network of fans who pledge to attend women's sporting events.[40] SheIS is the first organization to mobilize fans to grow women's sports. I am a member of the LPGA (Ladies Professional Golf Association-Amateur Association), and that organization joined SheIS in

2019. Along with the USGA (United States Golf Association), this marked the first formal addition of major golf organizations to the SheIS Collective.

Ever since the USGA joined the SheIS Collective, it has been focused on increasing attention around women's championships, specifically the U.S. Women's Open (founded in 1946), as well as the earlier U.S. Women's Amateur (which in 1895 marked the beginning of competitive female golf in the United States).

In joining the SheIS Collective, USGA executives and the SheIS Collective leaders are creating new opportunities to engage golf fans around tentpole events throughout the year.

The SheIS Collective also includes organizations such as the Women's National Basketball Association, WWE (World Wrestling Entertainment), US Tennis Association, Canadian Football League, and National Women's Soccer League, as well as hundreds of individual athletes and business leaders.

Following is an alphabetical list of the top women sports, and potential for earnings as of this writing.

Basketball (WNBA)

Overall, WNBA women basketball athletes average around $79,000 while the maximum salary caps at $117,500. The minimum player salary for players with three or more years of service is $56,375. Some of the more prominent female players are triggering a firestorm of debate as they are addressing the huge pay gap between professional women and men basketball players.[41]

The women seem to be justified in complaining about the pay discrepancy between male and female players. In 2018, NBA star LeBron James signed a four-year contract with the Los Angeles Lakers worth $154 million. The most skilled WNBA players make just a fraction of what a frequently benched player in the NBA can earn. Women also are calling attention to the pay model in which WNBA players receive about 25% of the league's revenue compared to the NBA, which pays players about 50% of revenue.

When it gets right down to it, no matter the sport, the amount of money available to pay players is all about ticket sales, broadcast rights, and how much money the sport can bring in from the fans. It's clear that some of the wage disparities can be attributed to the difference in how much the leagues bring in. For example, the WNBA only grosses $25 million in annual revenue. Contrast that to the NBA which, in 2019, raked in a whopping $7.4 billion.

The WNBA receives less money in broadcast rights than the NBA. Its teams play only 34 games in a four-and-a-half month season, which is extended slightly if they make the playoffs. By comparison, NBA teams play 82 games in the regular season for six months, while the finals can stretch the season another two months.

The most recent figures for the WNBA is between 4,500 to 6,000 fans attending per game, with an average ticket price of $17.42.[42] An additional problem is that several WNBA teams have had to move to different arenas, which can disrupt attendance patterns.[43] What this means is that there has been a move over the past few years to downsize venues that will save franchises money and provide a more intimate experience for the fans.[44]

According to ESPN, for the 2018-2019 season, NBA teams saw an average of anywhere from just under 15,000 to just over 20,000 fans attend per home game. With tickets costing anywhere from $89 to $100 on up, on average in the NBA, the money earned from ticket sales adds up quickly.[45] Just for comparison, during the 2019/2020 season, those numbers were roughly 600,000 per game.[46] NBA players benefit from a league that has been around since 1946, while the WNBA was more recently created in 1996.

Golf (LPGA)

The median income for all golf pros is $141,428. The top 10 percent of players earned a median of $1,320,900 and played in at least 20 tournaments. Median means that half of the players earned more than this amount and half earned less. Regardless, there is a huge gender gap in golfers' earnings. The top 20 female golfers earn $1 million or more. Further, top-earning and well-known players receive lucrative merchandising and sponsorship contracts. These contracts often equal or exceed a player's tour earnings and are usually limited to the top 20 to 30 players. Players also make money from speaking engagements, corporate events, appearances, instructional videos, books and licensing fees. But the LPGA take home drops drastically after that, as the lowest 10 percent only brought in $5,924 and played in about 10 to 15 tournaments.[47]

Gymnastics

When most of us think of gymnastics, we picture young women competing in amateur events. But gymnasts do compete for winnings, and some particularly famous ones (such as Gabby Douglas) have earned impressive sums through endorsements. Gabby Douglas was a 16-year-old gymnast who, at the 2012 Olympics, became the first African American to win the all-around competition and Olympic gold, taking home a cash prize of $25,000. According to CNN Money, she stands to make between $1 and $3 million a year in high-profile corporate sponsorships and endorsements from such companies as Kellogg's cereal. Typically, gymnasts will not make it to this level, but there are still opportunities on the international and national stage to compete for brand sponsorships, cash prizes, and awards.[48]

Hockey (NWHL)

The NWHL was established in 2015 with four teams. The league's inaugural season ran on a salary cap of $270,000 maximum per team and a $10,000 minimum per player. The players also earn 15% of profits from any NWHL jersey sold with their name on it. The league has since grown, and as of 2020 includes six teams: the Boston Pride, Buffalo Beauts, Connecticut Whale, Metropolitan Riveters, Minnesota Whitecaps, and the Toronto Six. Interestingly, the league is the first women's professional hockey league to pay its players, period![49]

Another interesting development happened on October 7, 2016, with the announcement that Buffalo Beauts player Harrison Browne was transgender (the first openly transgender athlete in professional American team sports). There has also been movement of NHL teams supporting NWHL teams, sharing facilities, and assisting with sponsorships, marketing, and ticket sales.

Soccer (NWSL)

If you are a female athlete considering which sport to go into, then picking soccer would be a better bet income-wise than hockey. The women's national team players earn a base salary of $100,000 per year, and an additional $67,500 to $72,500 per player as a salary for playing in the National Women's Soccer League. The women also receive health care benefits and a retirement plan.[50]

Tennis

Since Forbes began tracking women athletes' income in 1990, tennis players have topped the annual list every year, with Steffi Graf and Martina Hingis holding the top earners' spots for most of the 1990s. In the 2000s the top-earning female athletes were sister tennis stars Serena and Venus Williams, and

Maria Sharapova. Tennis remains the only route for women to earn near what their male counterparts make. Between 2012 and 2020, Sharapova, Li Na, Serena Williams, and tennis star Japan's Naomi Osaka are the only women to rank among the top 100 earners in all sports.

Recently, tennis star Naomi Osaka surpassed Serena Williams as the world's highest-paid female athlete. In 2019, the 2-time Grand Slam champion earned $37.4 million in prize money and according to *Forbes*, beat the previous record for 12-month earnings for a female athlete held by tennis star Maria Sharapova, who made $29.7 million in 2015.[51]

When you start looking at where the money is made, a good part of it turns out to be speaking engagements, endorsements, or YouTube channels focused on such topics as lifestyle.[52] However you cut it, the highest paid female athletes are all tennis stars. Why do tennis players do so well? The bountiful amount of prize money helps. According to Forbes, the total amount of prize money on the WTA Tour was $179 million in 2019. That trounces any other women's sport. The popularity of women's tennis also drives endorsement totals, which are also high.

Wrestling (WWE)

Don't mess with these gals (they call them divas)—they are tough![53] WWE is currently the most watched wrestling sport in the world. A report revealed recently that Becky Lynch was at the top of the list with earnings of $3.1 million. Ronda Rousey came in second with $2.1 million. Although female wrestlers out-earn most female pro athletes, when we compare WWE diva salaries with male wrestlers, we see a massive pay gap. "Normal" pay for a top WWE diva ranges between $200,000–$350,000.[54] But male wrestler Brock Lesnar's earnings have been reported as $12.5 million a year, and several other male wrestlers make more than $1 million annually.[55]

In the end, men's professional sports are more widely viewed, and more heavily sponsored and commercialized than women's professional sports, and this makes it especially imperative for female athletes to be frugal throughout their careers and make the most of the money that they do earn. I am not going to get into the politics of this issue—that is not my intent for this book—but it is clear that whatever the reality is for you as an athlete, male or female, let's make the most of what you have in your world.

2

Stepping Onto the New Playing Field of Finance

You wouldn't be reading this book if you hadn't already experienced the benefits of using the strategies of discipline, focus, and determination to achieve your goals. The key is to apply them to your finances. When you have financial success, as well as success in your sport, you can truly fulfill your long-held, hard-fought-for dreams.

Despite all the hard work and high pay that can come with a career in professional sports, the odds that a professional athlete will retire rich are disturbingly low. Nearly 80% of NFL players are bankrupt or in major and financial distress within two years of ending their playing careers, 60% of NBA players are broke within five years of retiring from the game, and some end up in bankruptcy court too.[56] The numbers are similar for those in Major League Baseball. The numbers are unclear, however, when it comes to female pro athletes (it hasn't been tracked like it has been for the male-dominated pro sports world), but there are many articles attesting to the fact that women handle money better than their male counterparts.[57] I wonder if that might carry over to female pro athletes?!

You don't have to be one of them. You have the opportunity to take some of that same winning attitude that got you to the pros and apply it to a different goal—massive, long-term financial success.

I know you have been open to coaching when it comes to sports, or else you would not be where you are today. As important as coaching is for the length of your career in sports, financial coaching is for the rest of your life. It can impact the rest of your life, as well as your legacy. In this book we'll look at what life looks like to manage your money after taxes and agent are paid, what you may have to reserve to pay your expenses every month, and we'll get you thinking now about the life you want to lead after you've left professional sports so you can live in abundance and comfort.

Maybe the biggest challenge for you will be figuring out how to increase long-term happiness in your life with having this money. Some feel that no matter how much money they have, they need more to feel happy or satisfied. Like a drug addict, they are constantly chasing that feeling that will continue to escape them if they rely on the wrong things to achieve it.[58]

Getting into the Game

Just like every great player has a bad game once in a while, no one can promise rock solid performance in the stock market every day. You can work towards rock solid behavior on your part, though, by being open to quality coaching on how to be efficient and effective with your finances, and making a goal of potentially maximizing profits from your investing while keeping risk and expenses to a minimum.

Maybe you see financial success as having your investments work for you, so that you can have peace of mind and focus on excelling in your sport, enjoying more time with your family and friends, and other pursuits that are most important to you. Possibly you envision using your success to make a difference in the world.[59] Maybe you want to inspire others to break through their own perceived limits and achieve greatness. The first step is to commit, take it on, step into the arena, and get on the court. Make the decision now that you will do what it takes to have (and keep) the financial success you've worked so hard to achieve.

The Goal

When it comes to achieving financial goals, the same strategies work in finance as in sports: focus, discipline, and persistence.

Focus means you are clear on what the goal is—to win! Trouble is, a lot of athletes embrace a winning attitude in their sport, but they don't carry it over to the rest of their life. They don't get involved in creating the vision for their own financial future, so they have no way to measure where they are or how much progress they've made. It'd be like playing in the World Series and not knowing the score, or which inning it is, or how many strikes you've had at the plate. How long do you think you could get away with that and still expect to come up with a win?

Discipline derives from "disciple," meaning being a student of some master or subject. That means you agree to the rules of engagement and promise to try your best to follow them. Be like the master teacher Yoda in Star Wars, "Do or do not. There is no try." This quote is a simple lesson in commitment and the power in giving something our all — not just giving it a try. Commit to say you WILL do your best and follow the rules of money management, as this is crucial for the rest of your life!

Persistence means that you don't quit. Even if you lose some money on a "bad" investment decision, you don't dump all your stocks and leave the market any more than a running back would quit playing football after one fumble.

Positioning Yourself—Make Sure Your Advisors Are on Your Team

There's lots of information online about investing and money management, but let's get real. Finding the financial information that pertains to your situation can be extremely difficult. As a pro-athlete, you are not average, you are exceptional, and so is your situation. You have achieved something most people can't even dream about, with a unique set of circumstances where most people can't relate, so you need a customized plan, something that will address your needs, the needs of your family, and help you take care of all the things that matter to you.

Antoine Walker, born and raised on the south side of Chicago, was a star NBA player formerly with the Boston Celtics. He had a disastrous experience with money. In an October 2014 YouTube interview he shared how he blew through $110 million with massive overspending and ended up in bankruptcy court.[60] Calling himself an "arrogant kid" who didn't want to listen to his financial advisor, he described how the pull of having all the money, and buying all the stuff, was just too much. He felt both internal and external pressure to spend. He spent like it was never going to end.

This was a recipe for disaster that nearly sank his financial ship. But he did turn that ship around. "It was my darkest hour," Walker told CNBC, describing the day he filed for Chapter 7 bankruptcy in May 2010. At the time, he had about $4 million in assets and more than $12 million in debt. His over-the-top spending combined with gambling losses and real estate investments that tanked in 2007 had left him with nothing.[61] Through all the trouble, he persisted in figuring out what to do about it. He declared in 2013 that he was debt free. Now he has worked to help young athletes avoid the same mistakes. He has gone on to become an analyst and consultant to a large financial firm, and he helped launch a financial education program for incoming NBA athletes. He says his goal was to "make a really negative story into a positive story."[62]

Contrast Walker with former Golden State Warrior Adonal Foyle. Foyle grew up in the tiny nation of Saint Vincent and the Grenadines, an island in the Caribbean. He was one of the fortunate athletes who made a point to educate himself and invest wisely, including becoming proficient at buying and selling fully-furnished rental properties in the San Francisco Bay area, as well as Florida, New York, and the Eastern Caribbean. While he was a player, he actively mentored and coached young athletes just entering the NBA. Yet he knows many athletes who ended up bankrupt and, in hindsight, all have said that they wish they had become financially educated first.[63]

Now that Foyle is a retired pro athlete, like Antoine Walker, he has focused his attention on helping those coming into the game.[64] Having completed his master's in sports psychology, he focused on retirement experiences of NBA players. Foyle said in an interview with National Public Radio's Arun Rath, "I think that players continue to make bad decisions in part because they're afraid to ask questions, and in part because people just try to take advantage of them."

One of his best "takeaways" is that the most important aspect of managing finances is to be involved and know where and to whom your money is going.[65] Large quantities of money seem to draw in those who would take advantage. In many statements about their life made by athletes, they made the mistake of assuming their financial advisor has all the knowledge and left all decision making to them, or they did not listen to their financial advisor at all. Not good if you want to keep your wealth! You need to make the decisions. Use your financial advisor to give you information and help you sift through the options. Foyle advises, "Write your own checks ... make sure everyone is representing your interests, and audit everyone, including your mother."

Here's your playbook:

- **Create a <u>solid foundation</u> FIRST**. Be involved. Know where your money is going, and to whom. Don't give control of your checkbook to anyone. Write all your own checks. Be careful who has access to your funds. Review your accounts with your (trusted) advisor regularly.

- **Prepare for Retirement and Create Your Life's Vision.** Think about what you want to do after your athletic career is over. Formulate a crystal-clear picture of the life you want to live. Set specific goals with target dates for when you will achieve them. If you are 20 years old now, and you have an average length pro-career, you could be retired before you turn 30! Realize that you may have another 50-60 years to live, so it's best to plan accordingly. Think ahead to this and seek out opportunities to learn which options might be available for you.[66] One of the programs being explored by professional sports organizations is trying to help young athletes by providing job shadowing at large corporations.[67] No one wants to tell you that you can't be a Hall of Fame pro player with a long and lucrative career, but even the longest athletic careers don't go past a person's 40s. No matter how you slice it, you need a plan for what happens when you retire. What do you envision for yourself? How do you want to live? The more cushy that lifestyle is, the more cash you'll need to set aside and invest now.

- **Determine to what degree you will help family and friends**, and what your limits are. Set unbreakable rules around this. Be cautious about committing to ongoing financial obligations. Instead of handing out money, think of ways of investing in the person you seek to help, such as funding their college education.

- Consider how you want to **make a difference in your <u>community</u>**. If you care about charitable causes, look first to those who have done it before and learn how to make a new enterprise successful.[68] Ask good questions—in fact, learn what those good questions should be! Options like charitable giving, needy populations, and community outreach efforts are all good—and all options that might be worthwhile considering.[69]

- Have your advisor and CPA help you establish **proper tax planning** practices to help reduce your tax burden. Even a small reduction could mean money in your pocket!

- It's also vital that you learn about **estate planning**, the "planning" that has to do with wills and trusts. Having your good fortune continue through your life, and building generational wealth enables your heirs, those who will come after you, to start out in life with a leg up. Protect that power by setting up your will and/or trusts.

PART 2

Keep and Grow Your Money

3

Adjust Your Money Mindset

"live with intention.
walk to the edge.
listen hard.
practice wellness.
play with abandon.
continue to learn.
appreciate your friends.
choose with no regret.
do what you love.
live as if this is all there is."

–Mary Anne Radmacher[70]

Money is not only about the "currency." It is about the emotions connected to it, and what people make it mean to have wealth or not. If you didn't grow up rich, one thing you'll probably have to deal with when you find that you're "suddenly wealthy" is a clash where your subconscious beliefs from your upbringing collide with the realities of actually having wealth. This, I believe is the root cause of why pro athletes who came from poverty, or even middle-class upbringings, can end up broke or bankrupt after they retire.[71]

The way to help avoid the crash is to work on your mindset. Your mindset is composed of all your knowledge, including your subconscious and conscious beliefs and thoughts about the world and who you are in it. Your mindset determines how you receive and react to information.

Here's how your mindset messes with your money. It impacts your perception of yourself and what you're "allowed" to have. Anyone who grew up "not rich" needs to adjust their mindset in order to become rich. And if you become rich, you must make yet another mindset adjustment in order to remain rich. If you don't, what you have gained will clash with the value system you were raised in. Any self-made person must at some point overcome limiting beliefs about what it means to have wealth.

Greedy, dishonest, selfish, cheater, user, shallow, rude, nasty. Ever heard those terms used to describe the wealthy when you were a kid? If you didn't, give me the address of your childhood home, because I want to move in next door. The typical middle-class mindset is that rich people are dirt bags. They look good on the outside, but inside, they're emotionally and morally bankrupt.

This is a way for people without money to feel better about their situation: "I may be broke, but at least I'm a good person." It's unfortunate, because it's this very mindset that makes it difficult for any self-made person (but especially the suddenly wealthy) to hold on to and grow their wealth.

With money, the choices that you make become more visible. If you look at the world through this lens, you'll see very quickly there are many, many extremely wealthy people who give back, do a lot of good, and are genuine, caring people. Poverty is no guarantee of virtue.

YOU get to decide what you want to magnify with your wealth. YOU get to decide to let go of any guilt, shame, feelings of inadequacy, or fear of being judged for being rich. It takes practice. You must be vigilant. Too often, the value system of growing up poor carries so much pull on the psyche that it can lead to self-sabotaging behaviors that can not only sabotage bank accounts, but also can sabotage a career.

Sometimes self-sabotage shows up in very subtle ways like getting injured, suddenly losing focus or motivation, showing up late, or getting busted for drugs or drunk driving. You may not think of this as related to your money mindset, but it is. That's how the subconscious mind works. It's not trying to ruin your life, it is trying to keep you alive, and it knows that you remained alive all these 20-some years by living a certain way, and by golly, it wants to bring you back to that state!

The solution is you've got to work on your mindset now, *before* you get into trouble. Pay attention to your inner thoughts about wealth and success. If you hear a little voice saying you don't deserve what you have, shout it down and assert, "I deserve this! I earned this! I am providing great value in exchange for this money! I am creating good in this world with my wealth!" or whatever works for you to get your mindset back on track. Eventually, your subconscious mind will learn the new belief and quiet down.

Whatever you do, be sure to pull most of your focus off what you think you might be doing wrong and recognize what you're doing right. Also, focus on self-care. Give yourself time to relax, eat well, and get sleep. Make yourself a priority. Prioritizing yourself will help to boost your self-confidence and allow you to be better equipped to face your fears and avoid self-sabotage.

Money Management is Also a Mindset

Another key component is to identify your values. Get clear on what matters to you most and make sure this aligns with your spending, and what you invest. As your wealth grows, and your life becomes an even greater reflection of your values, consider helping others reach their full potential. This may turn out to be the most satisfying goal you can accomplish. You will discover that going out to make a difference in the world by serving others brings the most fulfillment of all.

Not only are your attitudes about money set in childhood, your behaviors on how you will manage your money are programmed long before you cash your first paycheck. Children learn attitudes and behaviors from their parents' values and actions, including money management. Whether you knew it or not, your parents were your first financial advisors, and how they handled their money predisposed you to how you handle your own.

Take a moment and think about your parents and how they lived. Recall how they managed their money and ask yourself how well these strategies worked for them. Did they have a lot of debt? Feel stress over money? Was it hard for them to pay the mortgage or "make rent?" What did they do if or when they got a windfall of cash? Did they invest it, put it under the mattress, or go out on one big splurge and spend it? Where did they end up in terms of their wealth today?

This exercise isn't so you can judge them. They did their best with what they knew and what they probably learned from their parents. But, if you look at your parents' situation and say, "No thank you, that is not for me!" then you are going to need to consciously shift your attitudes, behaviors, and beliefs on money management.

Your Education Starts Now

Whether you learned good financial habits from your parents, or bad ones, you probably didn't get any help from school. Unless you major in finance, most schooling does not include much financial education (certainly not *before* college, and probably not even then), and so most people go forth into the world with little or no formal understanding of how to manage their finances. Ranking well behind Chinese, Estonian and Australian students in financial literacy, new research says over 60 percent of American teens don't know how to approach basic financial problems.[72] With no financial roadmap, too many people in the U.S. enter adulthood and make ill-fated financial decisions, like running up debt and possibly becoming entangled in even bigger financial messes.

Think About How You Want to Live

One of the best ways to stay on track with your finances is to get clear on what kind of life you want to lead, not just for now, but from now on.

Consider, after you retire from sports:

- Do you want to keep working?

- If so, for how long? At what age, if ever, to you want to quit work entirely? What do you want to own? Why is this important to you?

- Which other ways do you want to use your money? Why?

The 6 Keys to a Winner's Money Mindset

Key #1: Fill Your Mind with the Best Information

A big key to a great money mindset is if you base it on accurate information. Searching the internet for good financial advice is equivalent to walking up the bleachers at one of your games and asking everyone in Section 201, rows R-Z how you should grow your wealth. Day traders, get-rich quick schemes, "business opportunities" of all kinds abound. Don't get distracted or go down the internet's rabbit hole. Find a trusted advisor and get a real education, so that you can look at your values, your goals, your level of risk tolerance, and your timeframes to figure out the best course for you.

Key #2: Pick a Few Great Role Models

Next time you're in the locker room, look around and identify the seasoned athletes on your team who appear to be thriving financially. This won't necessarily be the guy with the Rolex and the Ferrari, or the one who's always boasting about a recent high-ticket purchase. More likely, it will be one who appears content and calm, with nothing to prove about their wealth. This type of role model possesses desirable characteristics that make them easy to look up to, inspiring their teammates to strive toward worthy goals. Respect those who practice what they preach. Many times, they will support worthwhile causes and show that they are willing to act on their beliefs. You will see them behave ethically and demonstrate honesty on a consistent basis. Once you've identified a great potential mentor, you might approach them to see if they'd be willing to offer some guidance.

Whether or not they become your official mentor, you can adopt their money mindset and apply it to what is right for you. It's never about copying; it's taking inspiration and quality input to refine your own goals and plans.

Even beyond your own team, you can look into the minds of the superstars in your league. Here's where the internet can be useful. You can Google the name of any athlete whose money mindset you admire and look for articles that share how they think about success and money. They don't even have to be living. For example, some of the best advice I've heard on being successful on and off the field has come out of interviews with Kobe Bryant. Also, reading biographies or memoirs of retired athletes and other successful people who inspire you is a great way to start.

Key #3: Examine Your Current Beliefs

Beliefs we have about money often don't seem like beliefs. We just think that they're true. Like I said earlier, if you didn't grow up rich, chances are high that you have beliefs about money that could limit your ability to create and hold on to wealth.

The first step to change is awareness, so I've outlined some questions you can ask yourself to help bring your deeply held beliefs to the surface.

Beliefs Exercise

- Where did my family come from, and what was it like growing up?
- What did I learn about money growing up?
- What was my family's attitude towards rich people?
- What is the hardest lesson I've ever had regarding money?
- What is the BEST experience I've ever had with money?
- What would I do with my time if no one paid me? Where would I retire?

Now, take a look and ask yourself: "Are there self-limiting beliefs here that I need to let go?" If the answer is "yes," know that the BEST way to let go of an old limiting belief is to give yourself a new experience. Do something different, get a better result, and build on that. Before you know it, you'll think like a wealthy person, and this will help you remain a wealthy person.

Key #4: Fortify Your Mindset with a Vision and Set Goals

To maintain a positive mindset, it's important to realize that it could mean you have to say no to something you feel like saying yes to. It helps if you start with a clear vision as a reference point, as well as set goals that you can achieve along the way. This can help you stay on track, even when you're tempted not to.

Clearly see a vision of where you want to go. Write it down somewhere where you can re-read it frequently. Remember to include your WHY. What are your reasons for wanting what you want?

For help with goal-setting try this "Lookback Exercise."

Let's say, with hindsight being 20/20 as you're looking back, ask yourself: What needs to happen NOW for me to feel good about where I am financially?

- 1 year from now?

- 5 years from now?

- 20 years from now?

Key #5: Protect Your Mindset

"If you are worried about what someone is saying about you—those words will take away from you what you are setting forth to accomplish in preparing for and trying to make the team or trying to make a certain spot. My advice is to have confidence and believe in yourself!"

~ Julian Edelman, wide receiver, New England Patriots

Don't let negative people drag you down. Protect your mindset against bad information and negativity overload. Keep your confidence high. Believe in yourself. Be in a state of constant improvement. And look to help others along the way. You can't go wrong with that.

Key #6: Don't Let a Mistake Trash Your Money Mindset

"If you're not making mistakes, then you're not doing anything. I'm positive that a doer makes mistakes."

~ John Wooden, American basketball coach and winner of 10 NCAA championships

Like anything in life, sometimes you're going to make mistakes managing your money. Don't let any mistake pull you off your vision. Look for the lesson and move on. Before you know that you're competent at managing money, you may find yourself slipping into feelings that are signs of a lack of confidence. Take note and get support from a trusted advisor to help you navigate the waters without allowing insecurities to hijack your progress.

Signs that you're feeling overwhelmed

- Avoidance: not spending time on personal financial issues

- Arrogance: being careless, coming at investment opportunities with an "I know" attitude.

Finally, there is one more thought on money mindset that I believe is a vital piece to lasting happiness...

Money Doesn't Make You Happy, You Do.

"Wealth is only a source of happiness when it is used to do good for others."

~ Denis Waitley

Rich people get depressed, just like anyone else. True, there's no evidence that money makes you unhappy. But the adage that money doesn't buy happiness holds true. My grandma was right when she told me to value health and friends over money and stuff. Perhaps someone in your life has shared the same wisdom with you.

Those that learn to master wealth find useful, productive outlets to do good in the world, as well as enjoying a lifestyle that few realize in their lifetime. Western culture seems to measure wealth from the outside, that "things" and "stuff" bring happiness. Don't get trapped in a perpetual-motion wheel that cycles through acquiring more and more and more, trying to use acquisition as a source of happiness. Sooner or later the happiness fades and you're left searching for deeper self-fulfillment. Discover what truly makes you happy and live your life in harmony with your deeper values.

Here's what I know for sure:

- The dysfunctional beliefs you have were created in the past.

- You can change the beliefs that no longer serve you and create something new, something powerful, something of great worth for you and your family.

- To change outdated beliefs, you have to create a vision for your future so powerful that it reprograms your mind.

- Take consistent action to find the mindset that will support your long-term goals—persisting through the inevitable challenges and ups and downs is part of building wealth. But those who keep their head in the game longest win!

- You are great just as you are. You are whole and complete. This information is coming to you at the right time. To be the powerful, impactful person that you are, you need to drive a truck through those beliefs that have limited your thinking in the past.

- You can make a difference, as many athletes have. For inspiration, look at what the Lebron James Foundation has done for homeless people in Akron, OH. Through the I PROMISE Program, the foundation serves thousands of Akron-area students by providing them with the programs, support, and mentors they need for success in school and beyond.[73]

4

The 7 Critical Principles of Sound Money Management

Before you get into investing, set yourself up for success by learning how to become a great money manager. You've already achieved awesomeness with your athletic career. Now it is time to be awesome with your finances. When it comes to money, you may have come into this chapter of your life a bit worried about how to handle it. Understanding these principles will provide the foundation for long-term financial success.

If you use a financial app like Mint, you can check your financials from your smartphone, and be on top of your green no matter where your team is playing. YES, you will be in close touch with your advisor, but you need to be involved with the management of your money and how it is deployed. Resolve to take personal responsibility for your finances and being aware of what's going on. This requires time, effort, and a little expense, but the payoffs are huge. Like America's first millionaire Benjamin Franklin said, "An investment in yourself pays the best interest."

Principle 1: Pay Yourself First

Despite your best efforts, you'll face unforeseen circumstances and emergencies. Save enough money and stock up on insurance to be able to weather extended unemployment, accidents, catastrophic medical care, large car or house repairs, or natural disasters. Increasing the amount of money you save when times are good can help you manage the cost of unexpected financial exposure and make sure it does not derail your long-term goals and your family's financial security.

Get into the habit of saving money by paying yourself first. On a regular basis, transfer money to your savings account even before you pay bills. Many banks will let you set up a recurring transfer from checking to savings through online banking, so you don't even have to remember to do it. You can save money automatically. Planning for the future means both investing for growth and preparing for the unexpected, so set aside money to invest as well as more liquid savings to use as an emergency fund to handle life's unforeseen expenses.

A good goal for savings is to have a year's worth of living expenses in the bank (or in a conservative savings fund). It can be the difference between staying afloat or getting into serious financial trouble when times are tough. Financial advisors would tell the average person to just set aside 10 percent of every check they get. But you have a much larger opportunity. For example, Ron Gronkowski was famous in the news for saving every penny of money from his previous year's contract with the New England Patriots, and he lived on funds he received from endorsements.[74] Granted, this might be unavailable for some, but it would be a good goal to work towards. It certainly isn't possible for every pro athlete, but there is a place in the range between 10%—100% that you can and should set aside.

Savings is a critical budget item. Always include savings into your budget. Think of the squirrel saving his nuts for the long, hard winter ahead. Having cash in the bank feels great, and even though liquid savings doesn't always make much interest, the point is that it is safe, available cash. You'll be able to cope no matter what happens. Save consistently!

Principle 2: Get Your Estate in Order

Even though we all know we will die eventually, it still falls under the category of "unexpected" because we have no idea when an end-of-life event will happen. With that in mind, as my mother used to say, "Take care of your business!" Get your affairs in order—life insurance, your will, possibly a trust, a health care directive, and designated power of attorney for both financial and medical directives. These are the kinds of things to work out with an estate planning attorney.

Principle 3: Spend Within Your Budget

No one is too rich to spend freely without a budget. The biggest companies run on budgets. Your pro team runs on a budget, the league you play in runs on a budget, and so should you! Whether you're just getting started in the world of professional sports or you already have a few years under your belt, setting a budget now can help you control the flow of money in and out of your life.

To live on a budget means that your expenses each month are less than or equal to the amount of money you planned to spend. For many of us this is a lot easier said than done. Because of your position as a pro athlete, you might have more opportunities to overspend than the average Joe, so having and living by a budget could go a long way to helping you keep expenses under control.

The first step to creating a budget is to figure out where you are. You've got to know your net worth—how much you have, what you owe, and your monthly expenses. Since as a pro athlete, your income may come from multiple sources at different times, you might not know exactly when you're getting paid or how much, and you might not be aware of which taxes have been withheld and which ones you still owe. You can see how easy it can be to spend your next check before you even get it!

If you came to the pros straight out of college, were you paying your bills or was someone else doing it for you? The way ordinary monthly expenses add up can be a shock to someone who isn't used to paying them. You might have to adjust your expectations and grow into the habit of managing this area of life. When you formulate your budget, you get to figure out what that all those budget numbers will be.

Once you have the budget figured out, the hardest part is sticking to it. Review and refine your budget on a regular basis. Make sure it reflects your current situation. Especially revisit it and make adjustments after major events, like the birth of a child, a marriage, or a trade. Setting a budget and making contingency plans for when things may go wrong may help you maintain acceptable income for the rest of your life.

Principle 4: Limit Debt

Sticking to your budget is the key to limiting debt. My overall recommendation on debt is to avoid it with few exceptions. The best way to ensure that you either overcome debt or avoid it in the first place is to never spend more than you make. If going into debt seems to be the best option, stick to financing items that retain or grow in value over time, like real estate and education, and possibly a new business. Avoid going into debt to acquire any depreciating asset, like an automobile. And try to buy cars a year old to avoid the massive "new car" hit once you drive off the lot!

With real estate, if you buy right, then you will have a good chance the property will appreciate in value. With education, the knowledge you gain will help you access opportunities that require the knowledge you attained. If you are buying into or starting a business, that too can be a good thing to finance, as long as you have a clear plan to pay it back. No matter the reason for borrowing funds, never borrow more than you KNOW you can pay back. And when investing in a business, never put in more than you can afford to lose.

I learned this the hard way several years ago with a commercial real estate venture that I was in. The builders mismanaged the building and it went under. The bank came after us investors first. Only after a lot of money spent on attorneys was this nightmare settled—an expensive lesson!

With credit cards and car loans, every penny of debt is money flushed down the drain. In the case of cars, all but a few models depreciate to zero eventually and require more in repairs and finance charges than can be reasonably expected to be returned to the owner upon being sold. With ultra-high interest rates, credit cards can quickly cause your spending to get out of control with a long road back to being debt free. Also, be wary of letting others use your cards. No matter who charged it, you owe it. Rookie pro athletes might enjoy a period of financial freedom with little debt, but credit offers will come rolling in, and can be tempting. New cars, credit cards, furnishing a big new house, or anything else that you can't afford in cash seems within reach if someone is willing to extend credit to you. Every new debt equals a new monthly payment. It's easy to fall prey to the promise of things that you want in exchange for small payments. Be wary of plastic. Be wary of running up huge credit card bills before you've got a handle on what your monthly budget might be. You may be surprised how many will be willing to extend huge amounts of credit to you, knowing that you have a nice big contract coming down the road.[75]

One easy way to control how much money you spend on credit is to have one credit card with a spending limit that matches your monthly budget for "fun money." You max it out, and you're done for that month. You don't use another card. You pay the balance in full each month through an autopay online or with checks that come straight out of your bank account. Maybe you have felt a little short on cash after a fun weekend, and after reflecting about it, not comfortable with where things seem to be. More money, even a LOT more, won't necessarily solve financial difficulties if you've allowed yourself to get in over your head with no idea where your financial moorings are.

A Comment on Bankruptcy: Another reality and follow-up to the discussion on credit cards is if this goes to the extreme, it can mean bankruptcy. When and if a star athlete declares bankruptcy, and then continues playing, whatever the salary or contract might be, the paychecks will most likely be directed to pay off obligations to debtors.[76] Tell yourself right now that you won't ever go down that road. And what a bummer if you are cut from the team for any reason, and then have financial issues to deal with! There are statistics that show that there are way too many players who wind up declaring bankruptcy not all that long after their playing days are finished. Many of these athletes had earned tens of millions of dollars during their careers, but the fact that they wound up filing for bankruptcy anyway shows that the "buy now, worry later" attitude has the potential to extend far beyond just the pro athlete teams.[77]

Principle 5: Track and Pay Your Taxes

When it comes to financial obligations, the three biggest ways pro athletes get into trouble are credit card debt, child support, and taxes.[78] The biggest nuisance, and pretty much the one that none of us can avoid, is taxes. There are two financial obligations that you can never escape, not even by bankruptcy, and they are child support and taxes.

Professional athletes are required to pay taxes in the states they play in. Let that sink in. Athletes are typically ill-prepared for this fact of life, and often fail to set money aside to take care of it. Professional sports organizations started noticing this issue, and in many cases, began helping players set aside funds. Still, it can get complicated because some states and cities impose income taxes on professional athletes based on their appearances in the different tax jurisdictions (including game days and maybe practice days, too). This is the so-called Jock Tax. A few states simply divide the number of games played in the state by the number of games in the season and base the Jock Tax bill on the resulting percentage of the athlete's salary. There is often lots of back-and-forth between the state and the athlete regarding exactly how much tax is actually owed. An athlete who doesn't have great advisors could easily get into hot water with the Jock Tax. The only states without a Jock Tax are Florida, Tennessee, Texas, Washington and Washington, D.C. All athletes have what's called a domicile, or a primary residence, which is one reason so many athletes choose to live in states with low- or no-income taxes.

Pro athletes with substantial income from non-salary sources, such as endorsements and personal appearances, need to be aware that often there's no withholding on this type of income because the sponsor is hiring you as a contracted employee. If you don't file accurate returns and pay the necessary taxes, big problems can result. So regardless of how this looks for you, if you don't pay, eventually the IRS will catch up with you. Beware of getting yourself in a really big hole that can be nearly impossible to get out of!

When possible, speak to tax and legal professionals before you sign a deal or get paid to find out what your tax obligations are likely to be. This way you can limit any liabilities that could surprise you.

Principle 6: Put Your Money Where the Growth Is

Money management advice is everywhere you turn these days. News programs, business news cable channels, online financial sites, and even your friends and family are eager to share their opinions about how you should manage your money. But despite all the latest tips and new ideas, sound money management rules *never* change. The most important thing to understand is that you cannot save your way to wealth. You have got to take some of that money and invest it in appreciating assets.

A regular savings account usually pays little to no interest, which means, when you factor in inflation, it's a depreciating asset. For example, while $1 bought you a gallon of gasoline in 1990, today that same gallon of gas could cost up to $5 depending on what brand you buy, what vacation hot spots you may visit, or what area you live in.

Let's look at another example of the difference between investing in an appreciating asset and buying a depreciating asset, this time from pro sports.

Example 1: *Russell Wilson Buys Amazon Stock for His Offensive Line—December 2019*[79]

After he agreed to his $140 million contract (roughly April 16, 2019), Wilson purchased $12,000 worth of stock in Amazon for each of the 13 members of the Seahawks offensive line. He'd bought it sometime in the 6-month period before Christmas Day. Let's just average it at 6.5 shares roughly at $1,846.15 stock price, which means he spent $12,000/person x 13 = $156,000.

Let's say that the stock price, just to make a point about this, has gone up to somewhere in the neighborhood of $3,350 per share. We're not picking any particular day–this is just to show the value down the road. Actually, because of the way the stock market behaves, there is just as much chance of the stock price being slashed in half if something happens to the company. But be that as it is right now, let's go with $3,350 per share. If you then had 6.5 shares, that would be $3,350 x 6.5 shares = a $21,775.00 value for each player now. No matter where it is on this particular day that you are reading this, the point is that it has gone UP, a $12,000 investment has turned into almost $22,000. At least for now! This is an example of an appreciating asset.

Example 2: *Tom Brady Bought His OL New Cars—August 2008*[80]

Brady showed his offensive line his generosity by buying them each an Audi Q7 SUV, valued at $42,000 at the time, meaning if he paid the sticker price, he spent $546,000 for 13 cars (I bet you he didn't). Today, a 2008 Audi would be worth about $5,000. This is an example of a depreciating asset.

Again, this example of gift choice is neither good nor bad (both Russell and Tom were being very generous), it just serves the purpose of showing the difference between an asset that has a chance to rise in value (it doesn't always but this was a good example of one that has really appreciated) versus one which will surely depreciate. Russell's stock gift will hopefully continue to gain value, and Tom's cars lost value the moment they were driven off the lot plus they need to be maintained. We still like our cars, though!

It's commonly known that investing in stocks (a partial ownership in a public company) can be one of the best ways to not only keep pace with inflation but to grow your wealth. Remember, there are no guarantees.

Principle 7: Donations

It usually takes money to be charitable, and now that you have it, this can be something you may never have been able to consider before. Churches, charities, foundations and other organizations all have one thing in common—they require money from outsiders to survive. Before you go deep into this area, get some advice from your tax and financial advisors. Your goal may be to reach young people by delivering unique experiences and/or innovative educational opportunities but consider how you will go about this. Not all "gifts" are free. Running a charitable foundation is every bit a business, and needs to be run in an efficient, businesslike manner, keeping your money management rules at the forefront.

5

What's Your Investing Style?

In my work, I've seen that when it comes to investing style, people generally fall into one of three categories: sideliners, gamblers, and investors. You can probably guess which one gets the best outcomes, but it's still useful to take a look at the three different ways people may behave around investing and how it impacts them. As you read, see if you can identify your style so far and if there's a style you'd like to adopt. You will see within these three types that one of the biggest differentiators is an investor's tolerance for risk.

Understanding Risk

Before you invest, it's good to know what risk means to you. Not everyone is tolerant of the ups and downs of the market. Look at what your risk tolerance is, and what you think your personality is when it comes to how much risk you should take. Are you a risk- taker in general? Do you think you are pretty conservative? How much risk is OK with you?

The key to understanding ROI, or return on investments, is that the more you risk, the better the return *should, or could,* be, but it can also mean a greater potential for loss. This is called a risk-return trade-off. Investments, like stocks and bonds that have a higher rate of return, often have a higher risk of losing the principal that you invested. Investments like certificates of deposit and money market accounts with a lower rate of return have a lower risk of losing principal. Since no one knows the future, you cannot be 100 percent sure any investment will do well. As you will see when you read about these three investor types, there are extremes in risk tolerance, and you can find a happy medium that fits your personality.

Sideliners

A sideliner is someone who refuses to get in the game. They are the most risk averse of the three types. Some have a severe distrust of banks and financial institutions. They might hide money under their mattress or buy gold and silver bars and bury them in the yard rather than trust a bank. Investing in gold or silver can be fine, but it lacks the diversification and spreading of risk that you can achieve investing in stocks. As to placing buried treasure in the yard, you will receive back absolutely no interest, plus you may forget where you buried it (that's a joke).

The sideliner who trusts the bank but not the market will put money into CDs and other secure checking and savings accounts, but they won't invest in the stock market. They're afraid. They are sure that they will fail. True, their money is most likely "safe" in an FDIC insured bank, but at what cost? Because of inflation and their unwillingness to take even a calculated risk, sideliners are headed for a future that will become increasingly difficult. Ironically, although for the people who refuse to get into investing in stocks to avoid the risk of losing their money, staying on the sidelines guarantees loss of wealth. Inflation eats away at any cash savings, as it requires you to spend more on everyday needs. This makes you vulnerable to the inevitable changes and challenges that life brings. Over time, as costs rise, the value of your secure little nest egg diminishes, your spending power weakens, and your ability to support your lifestyle withers away.

My message to the sideliner is this: No matter what the market is doing today, and no matter what is going on in your life, being invested can be critical to your long-term success. I know it seems tempting to think "I'll get in when things are more stable." The problem is that markets are never static. They need to have ups and downs. It is what provides the opportunity to experience gains. By waiting to educate yourself on this issue, all you do is weaken your ability to partake of the growth that is occurring. Worst case, you wait it out until it is too late, when you can't afford to live the lifestyle you want with the money you have, and stock prices have already skyrocketed from where they were when you opened that CD. Your problem is that you just don't know how to access what the market will do, how to approach this, or who to trust.

Like any game, you've got to be in it to win it. Investing is no different. By sitting it out on the bench, sideliners miss the opportunities to build massive wealth and secure their futures. Here are a couple of opportunities that if you choose to be a sideliner, you'll never receive.

Opportunity 1: Growing Your Money and Inflation

A bank only offers nominal interest rates that don't even make up for inflation. So, by keeping your money in a bank, over time you're losing money. In contrast, your investment portfolio counts on prices remaining relatively stable. Slight inflation, for example the Federal Reserve's 2 percent target, seems to be a useful zone for maximizing economic growth incentives for businesses and consumers. Slight deflation is more painful than slight inflation, as even modest price declines quickly feed into a 'wait until tomorrow' attitude for buying.

The real question centers on how to determine when inflation will rear its ugly head again. What would be the steps necessary to protect your net worth from the consequences?

The lesson to learn is that inflation, when it happens, happens fast and then burns itself out after a few years as consumers lack the money to keep pushing prices higher. Our current experience could be different as the amount of money created is larger than any time in modern history. But even a little inflation will outpace what you earn with a basic savings account. Looking forward, and thinking about those lessons from history, set a goal to stay ahead of inflation using wide, global diversification in the stock market.

Let's examine the S&P 500. The Standard & Poor's 500 Index is a grouping of the 500 largest stocks issued by big companies, many of whom you know well. The market value of the companies is reflected by the stock price and the number of shares of the company. It is seen as a leading indicator of U.S. equities and it is considered representative of the entire market because it includes a significant portion of the total value of the market. The 500 included companies (which can and do change) of the S&P 500 index have a wide range of market cap (value)— from nearly $1 trillion down to $1 billion. If you look at the long-term performance of the S&P 500, you will see statistics of around 9%—10% growth. Even though day-by-day the prices of individual stocks can rise and fall, over the long haul, these assets tend to rise.

Looking at historical statistics for the nearly five years from February 27, 2009 (close to the bottom of the 2008 crash) to February 21, 2014, we notice this interesting fact. During that time, the S&P 500 index grew from the near market bottom of 735 to roughly 1,836 by an average annual growth rate of 20 percent. This growth is way beyond the annual inflation rate which averaged less than 6 percent throughout the whole period. The excess return of 14 percent is the value that was created by having money invested in the stock market. That is the kind of money that may build your net worth and grow your wealth.

In another example, if you got into the stock market in 2008 when everyone else was leaving, and you bought 1000 shares of one of the S&P companies like Walt Disney ($30/share then) that would have been an investment of $30,000. Those 1000 shares have appreciated a lot (but always remember that companies that go up, can also come way down, or out, like Enron or WorldCom). Those original shares would be worth about $188,000 in value today (if you take an example $188/share). That would be a net gain of $158,000 in this example. Even though I am giving you some examples of individual stocks, remember that holding an investment in a single stock is incredibly risky. My feeling is that the way to go is to be widely diversified, as we just don't know which companies are going to do well long term, and which ones will go bust.

Opportunity 2: Receive Dividends

While not all stocks offer dividends, those that do pay dividends deliver annual payments to the investor's account. A dividend is defined as a payment made by a corporation to its shareholders. Usually, these payouts are made in cash (called "cash dividends"), but sometimes companies will also distribute stock dividends, where additional stock shares are distributed to shareholders. These payments arrive even if the stock has lost value and represent income on top of any profits that eventually come from selling the stock. I often tell my clients to think of dividend income as helping to fund retirement or money to reinvest, as you grow your investment portfolio over time.

As you can see, by only focusing on avoiding the worst, sideliners are missing out on the best of what investing has to offer. But even with all the drawbacks of sitting on the sidelines, these folks aren't nearly as bad as the gamblers.

Gamblers

Sports gamblers have lots in common with stock market day traders. Both are looking for the next big score. They both believe they can predict the future, and it's common for both to fall into the trap of making decisions based on greed more than common sense. Gambling on sports and gambling in the stock market both bring out the urge to put down huge sums on what the gambler thinks is a sure thing and then lose it all when the outcome isn't what they predicted.[81] As you probably have already guessed, the gamblers also are the biggest risk takers—unfortunately, often to their detriment.

In terms of investing, the gambler is the guy in the E*TRADE commercials who is shown dancing with a gaggle of girls and diving off his luxury yacht, except the real-life day trader's reality is not nearly so glamorous. Day traders get involved in investing, but they do it all wrong. Typically, they've had a little prior experience dabbling in the market. They buy a few stocks and then buy some online training program or read a book on day trading, and then, thinking they have it figured out, they up the ante and go "all in." Pooling all their funds together, they start taking on more and more risk, putting it down on one stock or another, spending the day online doing trade after trade. They feel like they are investors, but most of the time they are really just treating the market like a casino—moving money from stock to stock in a daily buy-and-sell strategy.

While they're hoping to make a killing, unfortunately, this idea that you can "beat the market" through aggressive, active investing more often leads to losses than gains. If you choose this approach, instead of gleefully diving off your giant yacht like the guy in the commercial, you might end up back in the harbor, scraping the barnacles off the bottom of someone else's boat. My advice: Pay attention, not to the commercial, but to the commercial's fine print where it tells you the truth, right there in black and white: "results not typical."

Another problem gamblers have is after they experience losses, they have a tendency to hop back and forth between being gamblers and sideliners. They cash in their chips (sell off their stocks when prices are low) and lick their wounds until they build up the confidence to get back into the game. I'll be explaining this cycle in more detail later in the chapter. The problem is that missing just a handful of the market's best days can penalize returns big time. The chief mistake of amateur investors is they buy when the market goes up, on the assumption that it's going to go up further, and they sell when the market goes down, on the assumption that the market is going to go down further. But a savvy investor will rebalance (maintain a correct mix of assets). Remember that if someone is selling in a panic, there is someone on the other side buying at a great price.

If you happened to pull out at the wrong time (like right after a correction, when the market is low), and get back in at another bad time (when the market is high), and you happened to miss just 40 of the biggest up days in the market over a period of 15 years, your average annualized return would total -2.62%. On the flip side, if you remained fully invested in the same stocks, without hopping in and out, you'd achieve an average annualized return of 9.92%, based on the historical data. In real numbers, that means $100,000 invested and held in the S&P 500 between 2002 and 2017 would have netted $413,330 for those who left it alone and let it grow—even with the 2008 crash.[82]

So, push away from the table or the laptop. Save your gambling fun for the casino and set strict limits on spending there. Think about investing in terms of making consistent, responsible efforts to accomplish your life goals and realize your dreams.

Investors

The people who can benefit most and build the most wealth are long term investors. They are most likely to be the real winners. With sometimes a middle-of-the-road tolerance for risk, they think long term, they have a plan, and they develop the discipline to stick to it. As a result, investors hold 99% of the net worth in this country. Sideliners don't have it. Gamblers don't have it. If you want to build your net worth, you'll do what wise investors do.

Sounds easy, right? It's simple, but not always so easy, because while the best investors think they know what to buy and when and how long to hold and when to sell, most investors don't. Let's take a closer look at where well-meaning investors go wrong.

6

The Ineffective Investor Loop

P eople that happen to be advisors sometimes are in the same boat. The reason more investors aren't rich is because most people don't follow the rules in a way that allows them to play the game to win. They play based on their emotions. They have the best intentions. They are trying to be responsible and do the right thing, but they make investment decisions with their emotions, and that's a big mistake that puts them into what I call the *Ineffective Investor Loop*.

You know from your experience with sports that when it comes down to it, champions do not allow their emotions to rule how they play the game. Especially in tense moments, when your team is down, when you're behind on the score, when you just got a "bs" call from a ref, when someone throws a sucker punch at you, those are the times when you need to be the most determined to keep your eyes on the prize and not let your emotions get the better of you. It's the same with investing. The circumstances are different, and so are the triggers that might cause you to lose it and make a bad move. But, as you'll see, the *Ineffective Investor Loop* is a vicious cycle that's driven by people allowing their emotions to pull them off their game plan.

The following graphic shows how each step of this counterproductive whirlpool cycle flushes your ability to develop and maintain a wise investment strategy. This model describes a common cycle that a lot of people fall into—well-meaning, honest, otherwise level-minded people. The graphic basically describes the pitfalls I fell into before I found this way of diversified investing, but even financially educated people who should know better have fallen prey to these issues. Because the cycle is ruled by emotions, it doesn't matter who you are, where you come from, or what you know, everyone is vulnerable to falling into it. One of the best ways I've found to avoid it is to see the cycle for what it is, so you can catch yourself when you fall into it and pull yourself out before you do something you'll regret.

6

Sell and get out, locking in losses

Realize you need to invest

1

5

Lose money and confidence

The Ineffective Investor Loop

Get partial or bad information

2

Market correction or crash

4

Take your money- buy some stuff

3

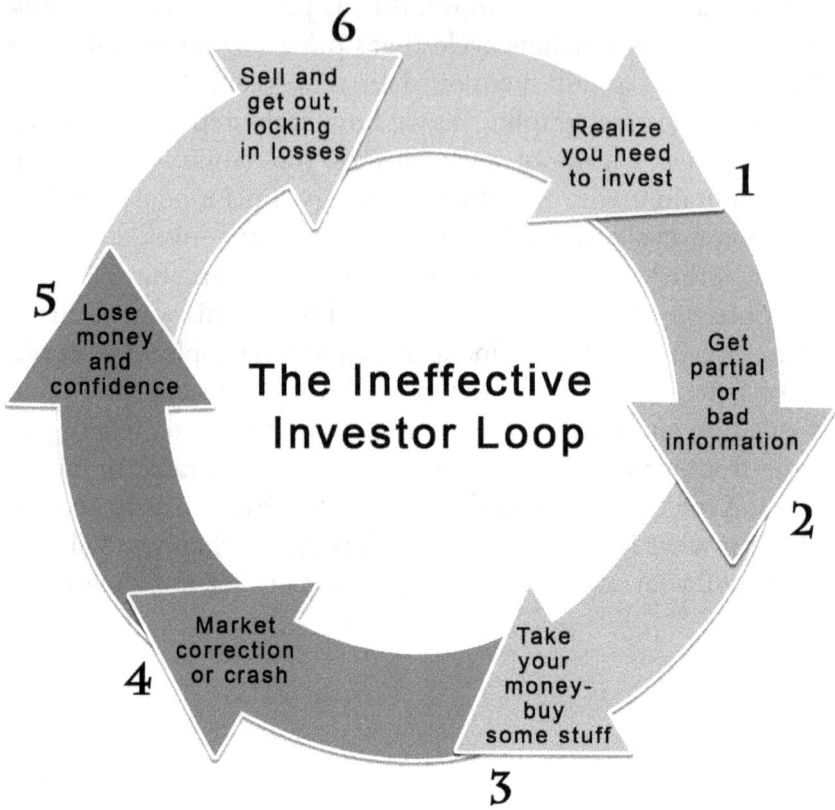

Stage 1: Realize You Need to Invest

The realization that you need to invest does not necessarily mean you're headed into the Ineffective Investor Loop, but it is usually accompanied by a sense of insecurity and uncertainty about the future. Characterized by questions like: "Will there be enough money to maintain my standard of living once my career comes to an end? How much do I need to save anyway? How do I know which are the best investments?"

The media and big investment company advertisers want you to believe their slick marketing campaigns which prey upon the desire for instant gratification or a fear of the future to sell products. There's no credible evidence anyone has the expertise to reliably and consistently predict the direction of the market, pick outperforming stocks, or select the next "hot" mutual fund manager, no matter which brokerage they work for. But many get so caught up in the feeling of wanting success that they fall for it, which is easy to do. On the one hand, you desperately want to be successful with your investment portfolio. On the other hand, it is very easy to be manipulated by slick advertisements for investing tools sold by those who want to sell products. All of this can lead to a LOT of confusion about what to do.

Stage 2: Get Partial or Bad Information

One thing hasn't changed: Gathering information and educating yourself has usually been a good guide for making careful investment decisions—to a point. However, the current information age has created access to so much information that it is easy to become overloaded with data. If you are new to investing, you may feel compelled to partake in all the information and read everything you can find on the internet, in books, newspapers, magazines, on TV talk shows, in advertisements, listen to teammates' experiences, and so on before you make a move. Indeed, instead of reducing fears, this deluge of information often intensifies an investor's confusion. It's difficult to try to wrap your head around comprehending the different options you see—in advertisements, on the news, financial networks and shows, in magazines, and the list goes on. Some of the sleezier ones will tell you that they can predict the future, and help you become wildly successful in a very short period of time. If someone could tell what is going to happen with inflation, long-term interest rates, share prices, and overseas markets, then they would be the most revered and coveted person on Wall Street, and the information would be kept secret for a very select few, high-level investors.

Everyone wishes they had a crystal ball to forecast the future, and we are often asked to believe that someone has the information, power, and insight to do just that. You may be swayed by stock managers whose predictions have outperformed the market the last little while. These managers hope that just because they had some lucky picks one year, that they will continue to have superior performance in the future. When you look back at the actual data from previous years, their ability to repeat a great performance is dismal.[83] Several studies have been done and time and again, market pundits get it right far less than everyone would hope. In fact, it has been noted that pundits/prognosticators get it right slightly worse than pure chance. This can be similar with the gurus who try to pick the top draft picks in the NFL, and they spar at trying to achieve the most accurate NFL Mock Draft.[84] Obsession with finding who is the best at predicting the future keeps everyone entertained, but it is still trying to predict the future!

Several years ago, before I learned this crucial wisdom, I attempted to be a day trader and pick stocks, and I was afraid of making a mistake. I tried to forecast the future, I looked to gurus who happened to do well in the past, and I overloaded myself with new whiz-bang tools and information. Fortunately, I woke up to the *Ineffective Investor Loop* that I had put myself into and turned my thinking around to discover the principles that we are discussing here. Look in the mirror. You can learn the principles needed to be a successful investor. Just don't become a victim of faux "sophisticated" money "experts," whose only legitimate credential is their skill in persuading you they have an expertise that doesn't exist. The sad truth is that investors stuck in the cycle take bad or partial information and go and buy some stocks.

Stage 3: Take Your Money, Buy Some Stuff

Here are some of the most common, biggest mistakes made when someone thinks they need to invest, but they really have no idea. These are the issues that come up when all you do is throw some money at the stock market and buy a bunch of stuff. In this stage, there are several potholes investors can fall into:

No Trading Plan: There's no well-defined plan, no exact entry and exit points, no planned amount of capital to invest in the trade, no maximum loss they are willing to take.

Chasing After Performance: The investor is influenced by asset classes, strategies, managers, and funds based on current strong performance. My experience in the past was that if something was good now, I should have invested three or four years ago! The cycle that led to this great performance may be nearing its end. With my luck, it seemed to crash right after I bought it!

Not Regaining Balance: Rebalancing is the process of returning your portfolio to your target investment plan, or how much risk you want to take. In this case, you are buying some "stuff" and then NOT selling it. It can be tough, because this principle is about selling the asset class that is performing well and buying more of your worst-performing asset class. If you don't go through this process, you can end up all out of whack, and have a situation with a portfolio that is not performing well.

Ignoring Risk Aversion: This is the guy that doesn't look at his risk profile (what's that?) and see how much money he could lose if things go wrong. Never invest more than you can afford to lose (this goes for ANY investment, not just stocks).

Forgetting Your Time Horizon: Don't invest without an idea of "how long" it will be invested. If you are in your 20s or 30s you have a LONG time horizon, or in other words, you will be invested for a long time. Think about if you will need the funds you are locking up into an investment before entering any trades. Consider issues such as saving for retirement, a down payment on a home, or a college education for your child.

Not Using Stop-Loss Orders: (Another "lingo" issue) This is where your stock goes down, and a stop loss means losses are capped before they become any more sizeable (than they might already be). A corollary to this common trading mistake is when a trader cancels a stop order on a losing trade just before it can be triggered because they believe that the stock will go back up—more stock market prediction issues!

Letting Losses Grow: Out of control traders can become paralyzed if a trade goes against them. Rather than taking quick action to cap a loss, they hold on to a losing position in the hope that the trade will turn around. This ties up your money for a long time, resulting in mounting losses and a big hole in your investment account.

Accepting Losses: Here's your *Ineffective Investor Loop* at work. The investor fails to accept the simple fact that they are human and prone to mistakes just like the greatest investors. They let their pride take priority over their pocketbook and hold on to a losing investment. Or worse yet, buy more shares of the stock as it is much cheaper now.

Believing False Buy Signals: Sometimes there are things going on with companies that you just can't see. Sometimes stuff is going on that means the stock might not increase anytime soon. It's hard to have a critical eye, as a low share price might be a false buy signal.

Buying with Too Much Margin: This is where some athletes have gotten themselves in trouble in the past—using borrowed money from their broker to purchase securities, usually futures and options. Your losses can be exaggerated in a hurry! It can be easy to get carried away with what seems like free money. What can happen is you ending up with a large debt obligation for nothing. When you don't have the time or knowledge to keep a close eye on and make decisions about your positions, you can end up with your stock being sold to recover your losses.

Following the Herd: Don't blindly follow the herd, or investors you are talking to who are all excited about some hot stock. You may stay in a trade long after the smart money has moved out of it, and jump right off the proverbial cliff, so to speak. In investing, this selling behavior when panic hits is likened to herd mentality when a herd stampedes over a cliff. Herd mentality is one of the worst behavioral finance mistakes, and plays out when you follow the investing crowd. Herding in investing occurs when you follow the group, without evaluating current, correct information. To avoid losing money in the markets, don't follow the crowd.

Keeping All Your Eggs in One Basket: Overexposure to any one investment is the opposite of diversification. Ask anyone who worked for Enron, or WorldCom, and saw their entire investment, or retirement account, go away. Don't get emotionally invested in just ONE stock. Having a diversified portfolio made up of multiple investments protects you if one of them loses money.

Shirking Your Homework: Are you able to do your homework on seasonal trends, or the timing of data releases and trading patterns? The urgency to make a trade often overwhelms the need for doing some research, but this may ultimately result in an expensive lesson. I finally realized I did not have the time, or expertise, to deal with all the nuances of the entire stock market years ago when I was trying to do this on my own. You are busy with your athletic career, doing homework on the stock market can be a full-time occupation.

Buying Unfounded Tips: You may hear your teammates or friends talking about a stock that they heard will get bought out, have killer earnings, or soon release a groundbreaking new product. What about hearing about some guru who touts a specific stock as though it's a must-buy, but really is nothing more than the flavor of the day? Buying on media tips is often founded on nothing more than a speculative gamble.

Watching Too Much Financial TV: No good can come from watching Mad Money's Jimmy Cramer, in my humble opinion. NO financial news shows will help you achieve your goals. Spend your free time creating—and sticking to—your investment plan. If they really knew what was going to happen tomorrow, they wouldn't be trying to convince you! They'd be on some tropical beach phoning in orders for their own portfolio.

Not Seeing the Big Picture: Back in the 1980s, a typewriter company could have outperformed any company in its industry, but once personal computers started to become commonplace, an investor in typewriters of that era would have done well to assess the bigger picture and pivot away. Or think about Kodak[85]—they helped invent the digital camera, and then SOLD the technology, gravely misunderstanding where the market was going. These are just a couple historical examples of trying to pick stocks you could get emotionally invested in. Don't do it— globally diversify!

The Danger of Over-Confidence: This is the granddaddy of just buying stocks with no plan. "Beginner's luck" may lead you to believe that trading is the proverbial road to quick riches. Such overconfidence is dangerous as it breeds complacency and encourages too much risk-taking which may culminate in a trading disaster. From many studies, including Burton Malkiel's 1995 study entitled: "Returns from Investing in Equity Mutual Funds," we know that there's no consistent way to select, in advance, those managers that will outperform. We also know that very few individuals can profitably time the market over the long term.

Stage 4: Market Correction or Crash

Any of several factors can trigger a correction—disappointing earnings reports from big companies, bad economic news from abroad, tumultuous political events—but corrections are a natural part of the market cycle. Different research studies have shown that there is some kind of correction every 1-2 years.[86] Whenever there's a market correction, some clients call me because they are worried about the big declines and in a panic wondering what they should do. We always review the investing principles we have spent time on, and the coaching we've done through all the market cycles. We talk about how investing done in this way was built for times like this—that global diversification helps the investor to weather the storm. Remember to remember that normal market corrections will cycle through, and it's going to be okay. Think long term—and turn off the news!

Don't be caught in the *Ineffective Investor Loop.* Don't be worried about failing to capture the returns you were hoping for because of mistakes driven by fear, overload, and guessing what you should do. Unfortunately, when people sell on a low and lock in their losses, they have given in to breaking the prudent, proven rules of investing. When this happens, you for sure don't receive the rate of return you so much wanted. Investor performance (your performance in how well you've stuck to a proven system) does not equal investment performance (the performance of your portfolio). When this mistake is compounded by market corrections, or worse, big crashes, your investor potential for reaching your financial goals is significantly decreased.

My advice for inevitable market corrections that will occur throughout your investor lifetime is to do yourself a favor—sit back, yawn and stretch when the market goes down, and realize that you are in this for the long haul! Understand why you are investing. Be clear on your long-term goals so that you will stick to your plan.

Stage 5: Lose Money and Confidence

If at this point the investor is totally frustrated and fearful of the future, this whole crazy cycle starts repeating. Selling during a market correction is what locks in those losses.[87] You have now sold your stock at a loss, sometimes a big loss. The end result is not enough money and NO peace of mind, combined with worry, frustration, and anxiety about inability to accomplish all of your hard fought-for goals for the future.

Due to the way stocks are traded, you as an athlete investor can lose quite a bit of money if you don't understand how fluctuating share prices affect your wealth. In the simplest sense, investors buy shares at a certain price. Due to a stock market crash, the price of a particular share (maybe worth $1,000 yesterday) could drop 75% to be only worth $250 if something unexpected and drastic happened to that particular company. If you panic and sell the stock, you receive back $250 for your $1,000 investment. We do not know exactly when, or if, that is going to happen, could happen, or how long a stock could stay down.

If you haven't panicked, and you have left the money in the investment portfolio, there's a good chance any losses will be recouped when the market rebounds, though of course there are no guarantees. With the stock market's penchant for producing large gains (and losses), there is no shortage of faulty advice and rational decision making. As an individual investor, the best thing you can do to manage your portfolio for the long term is to implement a rational investment strategy that you are comfortable with and willing to stick to. Remember, if you are looking to make a big win by betting your money on your gut feelings, try a casino. Take pride in your investment decisions, and in the long run, your portfolio has the potential to grow to reflect the soundness of your actions.

Stage 6: Sell & Get Out, Locking in Losses

A recent Dalbar study showed how investors are their own worst enemy.[88] From 1997 through 2016, the average investor earned 3.98% annually, while the S&P 500 index returned 10.16%. These returns have been roughly the same every time I have looked at different return periods. You could look at these numbers in any time period, and my guess is that you would find the same data. The reasons are simple. Investors try to outsmart the markets by practicing frequent buying and selling in an attempt to make superior gains.

To avoid losing money in the markets, tune out the outlandish investment pitches and the promises of riches. As in the fable of the Tortoise and the Hare, a "slow and steady" strategy will win out. Avoid the glamorous "can't miss" pitches and strategies, and instead stick with proven investment tracks for the long term. Ignore any short-term market dips, and stay out of the *Ineffective Investor Loop*. Ultimately the slow-and-steady approach will win the financial race.

Just remember the fact that the cycle repeats. Once the sting of the loss wears off, the person starts to look at the market, get a sense of FOMO (fear of missing out), and they get back in and repeat the cycle. Because we carry our cell phones around all the time, this constant access to social media has expanded the impact of FOMO on investment strategies. Through many cycles in the past, the internet has made sure we are aware that large cap indexes like the S&P 500, Dow Jones Industrial Average, and NASDAQ are at all-time highs and achieving super wonderful returns, and we wonder why our more diversified portfolio isn't behaving in a similar way. You may think it is hard to be content with your diversified strategy when every media outlet is constantly reminding you how you are missing out on the stellar performance that could be obtained if only you had a non-diversified portfolio (maybe only the S&P 500) that invested only in the asset category that is currently in the middle of a hot streak.

When it comes to investing, FOMO is significantly impacted by recency bias (that is the tendency to think that trends and patterns we observe in the recent past will continue in the future). Our fear of missing out becomes more and more intense after the market has just experienced an uptick. If we take a couple of steps back, it is clear why we maintain a diversified portfolio—it provides the best tradeoff between maximizing returns and minimizing risk. Yet, it's hard when it seems like all your buddies are taking advantage of the latest market trends and you are missing out. Of course, changing your portfolio to try and take advantage of a run that has already taken place would be foolish, (as you would be selling assets with prices that have remained flat and may now be undervalued relative to the market in order to buy assets that have recently experienced significant growth and are likely now expensive). These are the type of decisions that FOMO can cause, and you would be wise to avoid this type of thinking.

We have been in this position before. In the late 1990s, people wanted to abandon their diversified portfolio and put a heavy focus on the technology stocks that were making all their neighbors rich. In the mid-2000s, everyone wanted to borrow as much money as possible and get into the funds to buy and flip real estate. In the early 2010s, everyone was wondering if they should sell their stocks before a double-dip recession began and use the resulting funds to buy gold.

In each of these scenarios we were hearing individual stories of others who had implemented these strategies and were doing better than we were. Of course, with the benefit of hindsight, we can see that changing our long-term investment strategy due to a fear of missing out on what was working for others over a short time period would have been a drastic mistake in each of these circumstances.

After the market has done well, recency bias and FOMO cause investors to be more afraid of missing a bull market than of suffering large losses. However, in these times, we need to remember that we are choosing a diversified investment strategy because it provides us with the highest probability of obtaining our financial goals while exposing us to the least amount of volatility possible. When the media and our teammates insist on informing us how we would have been better off placing heavy bets on the asset categories that have recently done well, we would be well served to remember that a diversified portfolio strategy will almost certainly provide us with the best chance to achieve long-term investment success.

Becoming a Successful Investor

It's impossible to give specific recommendations here on what you should buy when it comes to the stock market. The best advisors will help you understand your portfolio and how it is unique to your needs, risk tolerance, and goals for the future. You can minimize risk by spreading your investments across a diversified portfolio—meaning you invest across a wide variety of categories. The easiest way to think about this is to buy the entire market, all around the world. Studies have shown that diversification can be a huge part of the success of a portfolio. Ideally, go global.

Choosing how you think about this involves defining these issues. A good investor coach can sit down with you and help you determine what is true for you in each of these areas. It takes a little time and effort but it's worth it, as it can bring you peace of mind. With a clear Investment Philosophy, the confusion, concern and anxiety that so many experience around investing will disappear.

What is the Most Important Thing About Money for YOU? How people perform or behave in life correlates to the way in which situations occur for them. For all of us, this is based on past experiences and how the world occurs for you. What this means for you here, in this context, is to choose what you believe in. How does investing occur to you?

The most important step in determining your investment philosophy is discovering what really matters to you. Think about the most important internal values that guide how you use money. This might include love, family, family, health, freedom, energy, faith, generosity, happiness, honor, beauty, security, adventure, independence, abundance, recognition and any other priorities that might drive you. These values are at the heart of all of your financial decisions (whether you are aware of it or not), and once you identify them your values can serve as a compass to help you consistently focus in the right direction. This is crucial and central to all the other choices you will make with your money. When you integrate your goals and values into how you are going to use your money, you begin to discover what's important to you, and what your purpose in life might involve.

7

How to Think About Investing

I nvesting is a lifelong process. Instead of attempting to get in and out of the market at the "right time," staying in the market all of the time can be a fundamental part of success for my clients.[89] The description of how to invest in this chapter is consistent with what we know about how free and fair markets function. The kind of investing I am suggesting you consider is supported by the results of scores of empirical studies of 50 years of professionally-managed portfolios. Doing things this way allows for reliable planning and implementation of strategies that could be important for your financial future. I haven't always known about this way of approaching the market. A brilliant advisor and industry investor coach was the one who opened my eyes several years ago to how to implement a globally diversified, academically structured way of investing. It has been demonstrated to be a very thoughtful, structured approach to the stock market, and possibly could be one of the most prudent ways to invest money. Of course, the disclaimer is that there are no guarantees. All investing involves risk.

That said, the current information age has created access to so much information that it is easy to become overloaded and take the wrong risks. Investors feel compelled to understand all of the information that is available through so many portals and platforms—the internet, "robo-advisors," books, newspapers, magazines, TV talk shows, advertisements, friends' experiences, and investing tools. Indeed, instead of reducing fears, this deluge of information—the good, the bad and the ugly—often intensifies doubts about investing. I believe this is the main reason why smart people who want to grow their wealth often decide to do nothing. It's also why having a trusted investment coach/advisor is so important.

Here is what we do know for sure about investing in the stock market:

- When you're young, saving for something that's years away—like retirement—may not seem important. But that is exactly when you should start saving, especially as a pro-athlete, since your retirement from sports will come at an age way younger than the average retiree. The benefit of starting young is the longer the time money is invested, the more time it has to grow.

- One of the ways to give money a chance to grow over the long term is by investing in a wide array of stocks, in a lot of different categories. We call this diversification. If we set up regular, automated contributions to diversified funds, you can have monthly contributions to your portfolio automatically deposited as you enjoy your athletic career.

- Consider that you don't need to invest all of your money in an investment portfolio, just the part of your portfolio that's geared to long-term planning.

- Stocks and stock portfolios may offer great growth potential.[90] Evaluating this from a historical standpoint, it has been shown that stocks possibly can be one of the best ways to maximize the upside potential of your portfolio. By building a solid base of liquid assets (cash), it could be possible to ride out stock market downturns with no need to sell when the market is low.

Let's look at what's at stake here. The goal is to enjoy this success now AND have a bunch of money for the rest of your life. The strategy is to establish good saving and investing habits and set a reasonable budget for living—both now and after you retire from sports. Think in terms of a nice blanket you wrap yourself in—wrap yourself up with money in a retirement account, a savings account in case of a career-ending injury, and a trust held for access at a later date. These are the things that may protect you financially.

Knowing you have money for the future can offer a tremendous sense of peace of mind in the present. However, investment decisions are often complex and confusing, so instead of bringing peace of mind, they can lead to overwhelming feelings such as distress, worry, and anxiety.

What I'm about to share should help quell that anxiety.

I believe that the best long-term approach is to diversify, allocate assets across a wide field (meaning the world—many countries, many places to invest), and invest for a lifetime. There is no reason to get involved with short-term, get-rich-quick schemes. You can disregard media hype and continuous stock market updates, knowing that with a buy-and-hold strategy that has been well-thought out, you have the potential to possibly have the money you need to reach your goals.

Choosing how you think about this involves defining these issues. A good investor coach[91] can sit down with you and help you determine what is true for you in each of these areas. It takes a little time and effort, but it's worth it, as it can bring you peace of mind. With a clear Investment Philosophy, the confusion, concern and anxiety that so many experience regarding investing will disappear for you.

Becoming a Successful Investor

Your journey toward investing peace of mind has begun. We will continue on that journey by uncovering how your previous experiences with money and investing have impacted your life and your strategy for investing. We are here to help you get answers to your questions and help you choose an investment philosophy that supports your true purpose for life.

Two Key Questions to Ask Before You Invest

Before you make any decisions about how or where you will invest, it's vital that you ask and answer two key questions that will frame every decision that you make. They are:

1. *What is your market belief?* Do you believe you can pick stocks, and time the market, or do you agree that we cannot foresee the future and know that the market is random? This defines the method you want to use to create an investment portfolio. We are talking about a "buy and hold" approach to everything that is in your investment portfolio. What you are NOT doing is trying to pick stocks, time the market, or follow some guru who had a good year last year (their previous performance). With the help of your investment team, you include in your portfolio multiple types of investments like equities (stocks of companies), fixed income instruments (like bonds), domestic and international holdings, and growth and "value" (companies that are financially stressed in some way) to provide maximum diversification between investments.

2. *What is your investment strategy (the method you utilize to create a successful future)?* How are you going to approach this dilemma? How will you behave when it comes to investing? Sometimes this problem seems too complex to find a solution. The sense of discomfort that comes with not knowing leaves most people with the feeling that they

want a quick answer with a quick solution and instant results. This may explain why so many investment decisions are driven by emotional and psychological tendencies that may be inconsistent with long-term financial goals. Sure, you want your assets to grow to the point where you've accumulated enough wealth to meet your financial goals, and the sooner it happens, the better. Who doesn't? Yet this will only happen by investing money wisely and carefully.

Don't Try This Alone

To come up with the best investment strategy, you need a trusted investor coach to assist in evaluating your situation and help you come up with the best answers for you. Whatever strategy you choose should be revisited and reevaluated every year. This is a fundamental requirement of a trustworthy investment advisor— they will keep tabs on where you are at and will review things with you on a regular basis.

Stay close to your investor coach, as they can provide important mentoring. Periodically meet with your investor coach, either in person or over the phone, to keep you focused. Always remember, if something sounds too good to be true, it usually is! We are thinking long-term, diversifying our investments to minimize risk, and staying disciplined. Here is one place where having an investor coach who can help you keep a cool head and avoid losses during your investment lifetime can be of immeasurable help. Partner with your investor coach, create a sensible investment plan, and follow it!

8

Select an Advisor You Can Trust

"With great power comes great responsibility."

~ Uncle Ben Parker (Stan Lee, Spider Man)

I once overheard a stockbroker bragging to a man about the yacht he kept docked at the most exclusive club in Seattle. The man replied, "How nice for you! Where are your clients' yachts?"

One would hope that all stockbrokers would also want their clients to have yachts. But I don't think that's usually what is "top of mind" for stockbrokers. Usually, they are thinking about their commission and recommending the products that pay the best rate to them for the sale. The stockbroker with the yacht obviously has done something right in his investing world to get where he is, but one main reason he's got that yacht is all those commissions he's earned along the way.

At this point, you might be wondering if it is a good idea to invest in the first place. On the one hand, it seems like a wise thing to do. On the other hand, you might be worried about losing your jersey. We've heard too many stories of pro athletes who took the wrong advice and lost millions. But, as you will learn, this doesn't have to be you. In fact, I've never heard of anyone could have lost their fortune by working with an ethical, non-commission based advisor and following a sound investing and money management strategy, so read on.

I believe, in the world of finance and Wall Street, there is a vast conspiracy to separate you from your money. Here are the participants and how it works. The securities industry is the main player. They deploy legions of brokers who are slick salespeople, bolstered by huge advertising budgets. Their goal is to sell you a wide array of actively managed investment and/or insurance products which you don't need and possibly shouldn't buy. The worst products they sell are complex and hard to figure out (like hedge funds and private equity funds), which generate even larger commissions for them and potentially poorer returns for you.

The investment industry has become increasingly complicated, so finding a trusted financial expert is critical for your financial health. As a pro athlete, you can assume that you have a complicated financial situation, which means you'll need holistic advice on several topics like taxes, estate planning, insurance needs, and investor coaching.

Almost every week, I read articles about athletes and other investors who have suffered losses due to the misconduct of their broker. While the stories differ, there are some consistent themes:

- The broker engaged in excessive trading

- The investor didn't understand the risks

- The investor didn't understand details (penalties and illiquidity) of complex, opaque investments like variable annuities and derivatives.

The result is always the same: The broker and the broker-age firm earn huge commissions while the investor incurs huge losses.[92]

Challenges of Selecting an Advisor

At some point in this amazing transition into the pros, you might decide that managing your investments has become too complicated or nerve-racking. So, you decide you need professional help. Wise choice, but let's first look at what that means. Hiring someone to help you with your investments doesn't mean you look away and "let them handle it." Don't hand off your money to someone else and forget about it, EVER! If you do, things can go sidewise in a hurry, and you may not get the results you were hoping for. Pay attention to what is happening. Be involved. Know what is going on with your money. Anyone who tells you, "It's alright, I'll handle it. You don't have to do anything" should raise a huge red flag in you. Take it as a signal to run the other way.

Any time you seek to hire someone for your personal financial team, you'll want to look for the highest-level performance at the best price for the services you receive. These critical financial decisions will have a major impact on your future. Sometimes it's difficult to judge what makes one advisor better than another. Think of this another way, if you want to be sure your advisor is interested in KEEPING you wealthy, (so it is not suddenly GONE) and giving you sufficient information to make informed decisions about all your financially-related matters, you should hire the kind of advisor that's required to do this by law. That way, you can have more confidence that they'll do right by you no matter what. This means an investment advisor who is legally bound to hold your interests above their own. This is called being a "fiduciary"—it can be the highest legal duty of one party to another. Being a fiduciary requires being bound ethically to act in the other's best interests. This might mean being responsible for general well-being, but often the task involves finances— managing the assets of another person, or of a group of people.

Let's look at some of the ways people seek financial advice.

Referrals

You could rely on referrals from trusted friends or family. People are 400% more likely to choose an advisor who was referred by a friend.[93] Even with that distinction, don't blindly trust anyone. Put some safeguards in place before entrusting someone with your financial portion of your life, such as regular check-ins, reviewing the books, receiving reports on all the different areas that are important to you. Learn to recognize the people who can operate at your level of demanding excellence and engage with them.

Before you take their word that their referral is your best pick, you might ask your family or friend these questions and see how they answer:

- Who is actually managing your assets?

- What is their track record?

- Are you familiar with their background?

- How do they get paid?

- Are they legally bound to act in your best interests?

I know that it's likely there are at least a few "yes men or women" who are part of your entourage telling you things you want to hear that aren't necessarily true. Don't cave to the pressure to hire a brother or sister-in-law to do a job they can't handle.

Robo-advisors

Robo-advisors are all the rage these days. Simply put, these technological marvels are computer services that use electronic algorithms to build and manage a client's investment portfolio. It's popular and gaining traction. Many of the biggest investment firms have their own robo-advisors, including Charles Schwab, Betterment and WealthFront.

I am not a fan.

These programs require little human interaction. You set your parameters, such as your time horizon and how much investment risk you'll accept, then let the computer models do the rest. They're a low-cost, convenient option, but this kind of advice can come at a high price.

When you sign up for a robo-advisor, you are essentially relying on a computer database to customize and build your portfolio, hopefully with your long-term goals in mind. They may have a good selection of funds under their umbrella; however, it's unlikely they will have the full range you would have if you were working with an advisor who has the potential to customize and diversify for your needs. Many of these robo-advisors now offer CFP®s (certified financial planners) for an additional fee, but the planning they do is limited, and it certainly won't be a situation where they will know you. If you're looking for an ongoing relationship with someone who can guide you consistently over time, it will be hard to find at most robo-advisor sites.

Beyond the opinion of friends and automated advising, there are many other choices for where to seek financial advice.

Confusing Qualifications: Pros and Cons of Various Types of Advisors

It seems like everyone in the financial industry (myself included) has some sort of alphabet soup following their name on their business card. Currently, I hold two professional designations, the CLU (Chartered Life Underwriter), and ChFC (Chartered Financial Consultant). There are literally dozens of different professional designations and qualifications that financial advisors can go by and to the layperson it can all be quite confusing. Here's a quick rundown.

- **Insurance Agent:** These are sales/commission-based advisors, which can include an agent or some kind of broker/dealer representative. These people receive a commission from insurance companies and/or mutual fund companies for placing a client's money into its respective products. This type of agent, though possibly well-intended, will receive that commission whether or not it goes well for you.

- **Stockbroker:** Truth is, some in the investment world, like stockbrokers, might not be concerned about the client's outcomes (in my humble opinion). I hesitate to make a blanket statement, but usually it's all about commissions on sales. Being a stockbroker is mostly a sales job. They are tasked with bringing in money to the company. They get you as a client, and trade actively with your money, trying to beat the market.[94] The stockbroker "brokers" or trades stocks that a company sells to the public or private sectors. If you have seen Wall Street pictures on the nightly news, possibly you will have some idea of what I am describing here. Some stockbrokers are actually on the floor of the New York Stock Exchange, while others do it from behind a desk for a large firm. Their job is to make money for the firm. They must have a Series 7 securities license to sell individual stocks and bonds. Years ago, an investor needed one to sell individual stocks and bonds, now anyone can open an account online and make a trade, paying a commission to the company ranging from zero to under $10 for both buying and selling individual stocks.

Both insurance agents and stockbrokers are commission-based professionals. Often, that piece of the transaction is built in, even if you can't see it. Sometimes the money is clearly missing from your contributions (as in the sales charge deducted from the money coming in before it is invested,) sometimes it is not. It isn't so obvious as writing a check. Be sure to watch out for steep transaction fees. Those are a warning sign that your financial advisor might not be in your corner.

So, what is their incentive? It could be said, and sometimes this is the fear, that an insurance agent or a stockbroker who earns a commission each time he/she buys and sells, has some motivation to keep buying and selling, or placing you into new products. Thus, you must ask, who is this person working for? Not you. Or at least not you *first*. I do feel that many are well-intentioned, but in the end, the incentive could be in the wrong place, and it is looked upon as a lower standard.

Life insurance and disability insurance agents receive a commission no matter what happens to your money, but that is how insurance agents get paid, with a commission. Keep this in focus—your financial advisor should be helping you figure out how you can reduce tax liabilities, make sound financial decisions, and manage your investment portfolio to achieve reasonable returns over time, not solely on how they can up their commissions.

Fee-Only and Fee-Based Advisors

You as a professional athlete must understand that fee-based financial planning is NOT a regulated industry in the same manner as public accounting, the practice of law, or the selling of securities. Charging a fee does not make a particular advisor any more or less qualified to provide financial advice. In fact, when dealing with either one of these, fee-based or fee only financial advisors, it is important to ensure you are dealing with someone who is part of a legitimate professional organization—a lawyer, a licensed accountant, or someone holding one of the currently accepted financial designations. It is also advisable to ensure that the advisor carries liability insurance and can provide you with quality references, preferably long-term clients.

Fee-Only: This type of advisor typically JUST provides you with a financial plan, and they tend to be unlicensed to sell products in some places, or for some products and services. Some fee-only planners and fund managers charge you a bill, which sometimes come from your bank account but usually is taken out of your managed assets. These charges tend to be transparent in that you know the rate, and you know what to expect. Nothing is "hidden" from view.

A fee-only advisor can't fill their pocketbook by playing with your money. Their role is to plot out a financial plan for you. You then could be left on your own to implement the strategy. This is fine for tech-savvy do-it-yourself investors who don't mind using discount online brokerages to make their stock trades, but this may not be ideal for a pro athlete who is often on the road, needing to take time out to spend hours in front of the computer making their own trades, or figuring out which life insurance product is best.

Fee-Based: On the other hand, the fee-based advisor will also be knowledgeable about and licensed to sell products. There is no guarantee that the fee-based advisor will save you money or provide better results than a commissioned insurance-type agent. However, if the fee-based advisor does their job correctly, they should be able to help you cut costs, but this is by no means guaranteed. Also, often the fee-based advisor has a "minimum assets" to qualify to work with them. That means that if you are having them manage your money, let's say $1 million, they might have told you that $500,000 was the minimum assets under management that they would take on. Fee-based advisors charge a fee (1 percent is typical) directly to their client's accounts that are under management. Remember this is a flat rate. Many clients feel that a fee-based advisor/planner will represent their best interests first. BUT, let's look deeper.

There are many aspects to consider when hiring an advisor. Both fee-only and fee-based advisors are licensed advisors, but the first mandatory question is whether he or she is a 'fiduciary.' A fiduciary, like a lawyer or doctor, is tasked with or obligated to act in your best interest. Once this role is in place, you want to be assured that the fiduciary uses the industry's best practices. While fee-only and fee-based advisors are licensed to give you investment advice, they typically don't get into the realm of "Investor Coaching," which is a term for someone who has the ability to help you invest, but also looks at your behavior when it comes to financial matters, using a holistic financial coaching model to look at your entire situation.

Investor Coach

Let's take a deeper look at the difference between a financial advisor and an investor coach. A financial advisor, whether they are a registered financial advisor (RIA), financial planner, or broker, manages the money you've already saved. Traditional financial planning is the source of much of the distress that people feel in their financial lives. Why is this the case when it seems so logical to hire a planner to escape our financial difficulties? The root of the problem lies in the way planning is carried out.

At its worst, financial planning is used as a sales tool rather than a process to create more peace of mind for the investor. You've seen in this book why we can be our own worst enemy when it comes to investing and what you can do about it. Financial advisors are licensed to sell securities and financial products and provide specific investment advice that is tailored to your financial situation, age, and risk tolerance. This trusted position is often used as a marketing tool to sell financial products. The reason? To generate commissions on the recommendations. The individual working with the planner generally has little knowledge of whether the recommendations are in their best interest or the best interest of the planner. They also have little way of knowing whether the products could have been obtained elsewhere at a lower cost.

The majority of planners actually work for a brokerage firm or a broker/dealer and don't really work for the client. The brokerage firm controls what products can be recommended, in many cases. Some are also licensed to make investments on your behalf, while some may use an investment management company to do the heavy lifting of the actual investing.

This traditional planning process does little to educate investors and help them deal with the instincts and emotions that are at the root of the poor investment returns that they experience. You can tell if your advisor is helping you avoid these problems by asking yourself the questions about investing located in Appendix B of this book. We will go into much greater detail if and when we actually meet.

On the other hand, a good investor coach provides the "big picture" overview of money, investing, and wealth building. If done well, this will begin with a discussion of your life's purpose and what your higher purpose for money is. This can also, in some cases, include help with budgeting, saving, and tax-reduction strategies as well as investing strategies. The investor coach helps guide you up the investing mountain towards your investing goals, providing a clear step-by-step roadmap that teaches you about the investing process. Your coach keeps you on the path and help you avoid the costly mistakes that can send you falling down the side of the mountain.

In my case, I think I have the best of both worlds. I get to coach my clients, and I have an amazing team and back office that handles the details of a globally diversified portfolio, investing all over the world. The coach's job is to help you to create your wealth. We focus on your financial education, and your WHY around all of this, and help you build the skills necessary to understand investing and wealth building and to make informed investing decisions. My biggest role is to provide guidance and education, and help you manage the emotional, psychological, and behavioral aspects that trip up most investors and to help you keep your eyes on the long-term results that you are seeking.

A great advisor will think wide, think deep, and think long term. For example, I like to see a globally diversified portfolio of quality stocks and bonds that you hold on to. This is a powerful, disciplined, and diversified approach to investing.[95] In my opinion, there are three major principles, or platinum rules, involved with investing correctly:

1. Own equities (company stocks—all over the world)

2. Diversify widely

3. Rebalance, which means to adjust your portfolio to maintain your original desired mix of how you are invested. (This finetuning is where the customization that comes with having an investor coach can really make a difference.)

If all of this sounds too difficult, don't worry, it can be learned. In fact, it is very important that an investor have a basic knowledge of these concepts. This is all part of the coaching process. As a client of mine once said, "I don't have to know everything about playing shortstop to enjoy the game of baseball."

You may feel like you are in the stands watching the game of investing, instead of on the field participating, but I should also note that it is very hard to take advantage of an informed investor. Following this long-term investment approach means that rather than taking huge amounts of time trying to "beat the market," I can instead devote that time to serving you, my client, and creating real value for you. Over the years, with hard-won experience, there is a lot of wisdom that comes from helping clients deal with issues en route to achieving lifetime goals.

Answering some VERY important questions included in this book, I believe, is the key to having true peace of mind in an uncertain world. If you would like a second opinion about your investment choices, you can request a complimentary initial consultation at **https://bonitabellandersen.com/contact/**.

Here is what I have identified as adding the most value for you:

• Allowing you to focus on those aspects of your life which matter most in the knowledge that your financial situation is under control and need not absorb your continual attention (we just do regular check-ins);

- Helping you to understand how much you can spend each year without running out of money;

- Helping you answer the question, "What investment return do I need to achieve my goals and is that consistent with the risk I am willing and able to take?", using a prudent approach, working together to discover for yourself what is going on;

- Helping you determine when you will choose to work after your athletic career is over, if that is what you want to do;

- Helping you simplify your finances and consequently reduce your stress;

- Helping you discover ways to minimize your tax burden;

- Helping you avoid unhappy financial surprises;

- Estate planning, so you can leave your children enough to do something, but not enough to do nothing. (These are estate planning issues that need to be addressed);

- Protecting you from investment 'opportunities' which can sound fantastic on paper, but often contain unacceptable hidden risks;

- Acting as an independent third-party sounding board to help you evaluate the good, the bad, and the ugly.

We know that athlete investors (as well as everyone else) are falling prey to bullies both on and off Wall Street, who only care about *their* bottom line, not yours. Every investor deserves to build security and make smart financial decisions so you can comfortably enjoy your life! Your financial professional should be honest and demonstrate integrity. They should help you become an intelligent investor, be compassionate, and understand your situation and what you want to accomplish.

When important financial distinctions are discovered, it helps you maximize your financial possibilities which transforms your investing experience, empowering you to make a difference in your own world, as well as your community. You will have confidence in the future, have a sense of well-being, experience a feeling of success in your life, and feel like you have handled this important part of your life responsibly. Know what you value, dig deep to find the answers, be the best you can be, now and into the future.

Finding an Investor Coach

You assume that the best on the court have superior coaches who help them get to the top of their league. You are likewise looking for an investor coach who will help you get where you want to go financially. In his book, *Relentless: From Good to Great to Unstoppable*, author Tim S. Grover writes that Michael Jordan didn't depend on luck to be the best, he was prepared and in control, not relying on random events or mystical intervention. In his case, as well as yours, you are wise to value excellent coaching. It's what you do with the coaching choices you have available that will help you move forward financially.

When it comes to investing, there is no fast and easy solution. Coaching, however, is an indispensable tool that can powerfully develop you to be disciplined and prudent over a lifetime. This is not a designation or a license that the advisor receives or works toward. This is going to be an advisor that is also interested in helping you manage the emotional and behavioral aspects of money. This is the type of advisor that we feel you can look to. The big question is, how do you find the right coach?

Do Your Due Diligence

No matter which category of advisor you choose, you've got to do some due diligence and check them out before you invest. This can be tough. Corporations use methodical due diligence processes when selecting suppliers. In the investing arena, due diligence means you are taking reasonable steps to satisfy your need to know all the details of what you are getting into. You need to do this too. However, do you have the time and expertise? Probably not! Don't worry, I've included a list of questions that you should ask any financial professional you consider in Appendix A.

One suggestion is to check out advisors and investor coaches whose fiduciary responsibilities have been audited or checked out by a third party. This can be stated as a "GIPS-verified return" (Global Investment Performance Standard). This means the returns have been verified to be accurate—this is a big deal! There aren't that many investment companies that go to the trouble to verify their returns![96] GIPS reports on their website that 1,658 firms do this, and there are roughly 16,600 investment companies out there.[97] GIPS standards are a globally accepted methodology for calculating and presenting investment firms' performance history that are widely relied upon by investment firms, their clients, and prospective clients for ensuring consistency of investment firm results.

As an investor, you can rely on the performance presentations given to you by GIPS-compliant firms (ours is one of those firms). Claiming compliance with the GIPS standards demonstrates a firm-wide commitment to ethical best practices and that the firm employs strong internal control processes. What this provides you is confidence in the integrity of presentations from compliant firms, and the ability to compare performance across different firms. If a firm does not comply with the GIPS standards, you might want to explore why the firm has chosen not to comply.

Also, the state(s) where an advisor is licensed will have checked out that advisor before giving them their license to operate. They are audited on an annual basis against a standard of practice. An independent fiduciary compliance expert collects evidence of the advisor's investment practice history. The advisor's state forms that are updated on an annual basis will be available on their website for you to take a look at.

The bottom line is that while a fee-based financial advisor is a step in the right direction, it does not come without its faults. In the end, it is up to you, the professional athlete seeking help, to seek out an advisor that is best suited to your own needs. In many cases, the potential objectivity and unbiased advice you are looking for is what you will key on to make a final decision. Further, hire an auditor to annually review your financial dealings. By taking this wise move, you will keep apprised of what is going on with your financial life.

Surround yourself with an ethical, professional financial team. Key players include your financial advisor, a tax-savvy CPA who understands issues unique to athletes, and a trusted attorney. Keeping these three players with you can help assure that a proper system of checks and balances is in place to evaluate opportunities, identify risks, and provide enough perspectives to make informed decisions in any financial situation.

Qualities to Look For

Look for a fee-based investor coach who will ask you questions about your life situation and stay in close contact with you. A good investor coach can guide you to put together a portfolio that is appropriate for your situation today and helps you plan for your life ahead.

A good advisor will focus on protecting and growing your legacy, and first and foremost educating you by providing you with consistent updates, as well as ongoing financial education and tools to help track what's going on with your finances. The best advisor will act as your "financial coach" who helps you make prudent decisions regarding every opportunity that is put in front of you. A financial advisor can make a great shield. When your long-lost third cousin comes to you with a "no-lose" business deal, you can say, "Sounds like a great idea, cousin! Let me run it by my financial advisor, and I'll get back to you."

Any good advisor will also take very seriously their fiduciary responsibility to provide you with the highest standard of service, which sometimes includes having to tell you something you may not want to hear—like "No!" This includes helping keep expenses within reasonable limits.

Like you form a partnership with coaches on your team, form a partnership with your advisor, listen to them, be coachable and always be willing to put in the work. The whole team needs to have one common focus, and that is to reach the end result together—that you obtain financial freedom and long-term success with your money.

They will educate and inspire you, helping you contemplate financial issues using tried and true principles with exceptional quality and security in mind. This advisor will never stock pick, market time, or follow last year's investment guru, but help you stay disciplined and find success for the long term.

Your investor coach will avoid selling you complex financial products that are hard to understand with high commissions. They will also be "non-discretionary," meaning they do NOT have direct access to your money. A good advisor from a very reputable firm is going to know that you will need money sometimes or regularly.

When reviewing which advisor to work with, find someone who strives to create an environment where investors like you are excited to receive training and coaching to further understand their investments and the ideas they're built around.[98] What you want to look for is an advisor who acts like a coach and takes a team approach to investing in the market, building something that will support you the rest of your life. Just like you depend on your coach and your team in sports, you need a financial team with ethics, understanding, and the desire to truly help you succeed.

9

Long-term Success is Yours

Becoming "rich" is part of the American Dream; it's part of what many people define as success. Training and education in sound financial strategies can empower you to have break-throughs in your thinking and behavior with regard to money and investing and open up your access to a future that reflects your goals, values, and dreams. What few recognize beforehand is that becoming rich also means added responsibility—to your-self, your family, and, as a pro-athlete, you have a certain level of responsibility to those who look up to you as a role model.

There is more to successful investing than just creating an efficient portfolio. You, as a pro athlete investor, need to over-come the pressure to engage in frivolous behaviors that can hin-der your ability to reach your goals. This "dream" in the United States of America can be yours and is alive and well for anyone who is committed to achieving it. Those who believe in their future tend to invest in their future, while those who are con-sumed with stress, daily struggles, and a lack of hope, not only have less means to make such investments, but also have much less confidence that they will pay off.

Living the American Dream is all about YOU and your right to live freely and pursue happiness. The sooner you understand this the sooner you can start creating the dream life you've always wanted for yourself. Get clear on **YOU** and what makes you happy. Take stock of your life and define those things that matter the most to you. Then prioritize your actions and efforts into those things that will draw you closer to living your dream and reaching your goals.

A Higher Purpose for Wealth

It's funny that life gives you as many challenges as you can handle. There's just no "easy" life out there. Money doesn't equate to instant happiness. Overspending despite high earnings will create greater stress across the board—personally, professionally, and in business. Only by learning to master money will you be able to enjoy having it. When you become suddenly wealthy, you'll have an easier time handling it if you are proactive, become money educated, and build your confidence handling money matters. There will always be more to learn, always more to achieve.

Stack the deck in your favor. Managing your money for long-term success is achievable. Becoming educated about money management can be fairly simple, but requires some dedication, although maybe not at the same level as the effort to become a pro athlete. Do whatever it takes to achieve pro athlete financial fitness. The savvy pro athlete learns to let the money work for you, instead of working for the money. Indeed, financially-successful athletes have educated and disciplined themselves to set themselves up correctly, and they seem to avoid the most common mistakes that challenge athletes, namely rapid overspending and not considering the future.

Of course, it's not effortless! It requires focus and wisdom. Successful athletes deftly sidestep the servicing of huge debts for the duration of their lives. Another way to think of this is

"Care for your money, and your money will take care of you." No matter what league you're in, everyone from the rookie to the seasoned veteran has at one time or another had questions about money management and investing.

If you take nothing else from this book, bring with you these few basic attitudes that you can apply towards staying the course in your journey to financial freedom. My bet is you already are familiar with all of them.

1) **Energize your passion:** Passion makes work fun. As you know through sports, passion gives you the energy, persistence, and focus needed to overcome failures and mistakes. Use that same tenacity that makes it possible to overcome obstacles and pitfalls in competition to overcome challenges in growing wealth.

2) **Be persistent:** Persistence allows you to learn what doesn't work and continuously experiment until you find what does work.

3) **Be focused:** Success starts by developing a script of the life you want and desire. This script becomes your blueprint for success. It helps you define your long-term goals.

4) **Strengthen your work ethic:** You know how to do this. You put in extra hours to reach the elite level in your sport, and you love doing it. Now you can apply the same diligence to reaching elite levels of wealth.

5) **Maintain a desire to learn:** Continuous improvement requires a never-ending willingness to learn and stay open to new ideas and possibilities.

6) **Choose the right coach:** Every athlete knows what a huge difference having the right coach makes, it literally can mean the difference between winning a championship or ending the season at the bottom of pile. It's the same with investing.

7) **Practice patience:** This is one point that Antoine Walker made when describing how he lost $110 million: He wanted everything, and he wanted it all at once, and right away. The lesson that he hopes all athletes will take from his losses is to practice patience. Remember, investing is a long game. You're not playing this one for 48 minutes; you'll be on the field for 48 years.

In the end, if you always spend less than you earn, your finances have a greater chance of staying in good shape. Understand the difference between your needs and wants, live within your means, and don't take on any unnecessary debt. It's really that simple.

Many athletes come into their league with an inherent appetite for short-term, high-risk ventures. Player union officials are taking greater efforts to defuse that instinct, more aggressively promoting the need for low-risk investing and modest personal spending. Some think home-study courses on money management and offering investment seminars in league cities is the answer. But the task is tremendous.

Professional athletes have few peers financially. Those that I work with value educating themselves, are open to learning, and realize that they can always learn more. We work together to help you understand what your portfolio is doing and why.

Regardless of where you're at, understand that you can enjoy the toys, the trips, and helping people out, but pay your taxes first, then sock away a significant portion, so it is there for you later in life. Then you can enjoy the amazing lifestyle that being a pro athlete affords. Each individual situation is different, but it's important that you start. Your goal is to work on ways to set yourself up with income to pay your bills for the rest of your life. That, my friend, can be a pathway to finding financial freedom and peace of mind.

Appendix A

Questions to Vet a Financial Professional

It's difficult to vet a potential advisor to see if they're the best fit if you don't know which questions to ask. Here are some example questions to get you off to a good start.

1. *What experience do you have, and how long have you been in the business?*

   How does your experience relate to your current practice? Look for advisors that have professional designations like the CLU, ChFC and CFP. I would suggest that they should have at least 10 years of professional experience related to financial advising.

2. *Tell me about the qualifications and the credentials that you hold?*

How do you stay up to date with current changes and developments in the financial planning field? Those with professional advisor designations expand their knowledge and stay informed through mandatory continuing education courses.

3. *Which services do you offer?*

The services a financial advisor can offer is dependent on the credentials, licenses, and areas of expertise that they hold. The advisor must hold proper state licenses for selling insurance products as well as security products such as mutual funds and investment portfolios. The selling of individual stocks also requires a particular license. Probably most importantly, giving investment advice can only happen once an advisor is properly registered with state or federal regulatory bodies.

4. *What can you tell me about your investment philosophy?*

First you must have some idea of what your needs are, and get a handle on your level of risk tolerance, then find an advisor that isn't too cautious or too aggressive for you. Learn how they will carry out recommendations or refer tasks to others.

5. *Who is your typical client?*

Find someone whose services best match your needs. Many advisors have in mind a particular asset range for those that they are likely to work with, or will require you to have a certain net worth to take on your account. When you are interviewing the advisor, check this out beforehand to make sure that the advisor is a good fit for your individual financial situation.

6. *Will you be the one working with me?*

Some advisors are structured to work with their clients one-on-one, while others have a team of people that work with clients. Be sure you know who will be handling your account. You might also like to know what complementary professionals such as attorneys, insurance agents, or tax specialists are available to you. Check on the backgrounds of anyone you are likely to be working with.

7. *How do you get paid, and what do you charge?*

Most advisors will have an agreement that might be called an Investment Advisory Agreement, which should make clear how services are provided. This agreement will lay out the ways the advisor is paid, possibly through fees, commissions or a combination of both. What you pay will depend on your particular needs, and the investor will provide you with an estimate of possible costs. The fees may include the advisor's hourly rates or flat fees, or the percentage of commission received on products you may purchase. Sometimes the advisor fee can be between 1—1 ½ percent, sometimes the fee is negotiated. Look for someone where you get a smorgasbord of advice about almost anything related to personal finance.

8. *Do you have any possible conflicts of interest?*

Sometimes advisors sell insurance policies, securities or mutual funds and have a business relationship with the companies that provide these financial products. Look for investment professionals who agree to abide by a strict code of professional conduct and have an ethical obligation to put your interest first (this is the fiduciary standard).

If you're satisfied with the answers you receive about the investor coach, move on to more specific ones that pertain directly to your needs.

- What kind of returns should I get on my investments?

- How do I maintain my standard of living once my athletic career is over?

- How do I make sense of all the investment information available?

- How can I make sure I have enough money to take care of my loved ones?

Clues to Whether a Financial Advisor is Reputable and Trustworthy

A good advisor from a very reputable firm is going to know that you will need money sometimes or regularly. They will know what mix of stocks, bonds and other asset classes are appropriate for your situation and your life ahead. They will follow academic, structured processes. They will know that proper diversification is key to your success. Most likely, they will help you create a budget, and they will help you set proper expectations of what your assets can do for you. Make sure this advisor knows who your legal and tax professionals are.

Think long-term in all areas of your finances, and look for someone who will help you stay disciplined. Just like your coaches have advised you along the way to becoming an elite athlete, an investor coach can help you navigate your financial world. Avoid those who want to sell you complex financial products that are hard to understand with high commissions. Never give anyone direct access to your money!

Some athletes might think they need local advisors and accountants because they want to be able to meet with them "face-to-face." That is changing now in our increasingly global world. As a pro-athlete who could be traded, finding someone local today could become a problem tomorrow. Don't be constrained by geography. One of my colleagues recently recommended a financial planner located in California to a widow based in New York, and she is thrilled with her choice.

Bottom line—what you need:

- Find a Fiduciary (an advisor legally bound to put your interests first) who is a licensed, regulated, state and federally compliant advisor who takes mandatory classes on different aspects of financial advising

- Get a complimentary consultation

- Full disclosure of commissions, fees, and expenses (this should be in their legal documents about their company and their personal background).

Appendix B

Investor Self-Assessment Quiz

(When we work with you, we will go into greater depth with these questions.)

1. Have you thought about what your purpose for your money is?

2. Are you investing in the stock market right now?

3. Have you done any study of the economic folks that explain academically how markets work?

4. Do you know what an Investment Philosophy is?

5. Do you know how to measure risk in the stock market, as well as portfolio diversification?

6. Do you know what market returns are, and how to get that?

7. Do you understand how agents earn commissions and the related portfolio costs that are added?

8. Have you ever learned about the Markowitz Efficient Frontier, and where you fall on that graph?

9. Do you know how to build an investment portfolio?

10. Do you know the difference between a financial coach and a financial planner?

11. Have you created a Life Plan for your finances?

12. Have you ever heard of an Investment Policy Statement?

13. How do you measure whether or not you are having success with your finances?

14. Have you thought about the impact of the media and its influence on you in making financial decisions and how it can negatively impact you?

All investing involves risks and costs. No investment strategy (including asset allocation and diversification strategies) can ensure peace of mind, guarantee profit, or protect from loss.[99]

About the Author

Bonita K. Bell-Andersen is an American entrepreneur, author, investor coach, and financial advisor, focusing on the science of investing and financial education. Having been in the financial services industry for many years, she works with a team that creates educational experiences and utilizes platforms and tools that make Nobel Prize winning investing processes accessible to athletes and investors alike, with the goal of transforming their relationship to money. She believes that everyone, especially athletes, both male and female, have what it takes to build a financial future that gives them confidence in how they live today. It just takes a little bit of education and a willingness to take action.

The first time she really explored what Modern Portfolio Theory really meant in how to approach investing, she was hooked. It seemed obvious to her that this was how investing should be done, and she's been approaching the whole investment industry this way ever since. In an industry dominated by middle-aged men, it took a long time for her to feel like she could hold her own. Having spent a good part of her adult life in this industry, now she feels like she has something unique to contribute, and she feels very lucky that she works with people who respect her and are excited about the message she wants to share.

Bonita is the author of *Suddenly Wealthy*, and two co-authored books: *You Are a Genius*, (an Amazon #1 International Best Seller), and *Secrets of a Stress Free Retirement (How to Make Sure You Don't Outlive Your Nest Egg)*. She has been an entrepreneur her whole adult life, having founded several independent marketing enterprises while raising her family, and most recently founded her own registered investment advisory firm. She now has merged her firm with a former college athlete who also subscribes to the same investment beliefs.

Born and raised in the Pacific Northwest, she is the mother of three successful daughters and frequently spends time with her 10 grandchildren, as well as her additional 12 step-grand-children. She is a golfer and member of the LPGA, enjoying recreational golf as often as allows. She is also an avid scuba diver, enjoying adventures around the world, and now focusing her trips on coral reef restoration projects, her passion related to giving back to the world.

She has had many volunteer positions in her community. Most recently, she enjoyed being a member of the Development Committee of Transitions, a Spokane, WA-based non-profit serving homeless women and children. She holds two professional designations, the ChFC (Chartered Financial Consultant) and the CLU (Chartered Life Underwriter). She graduated from Washington State University (Cum Laude) with a BA in Communications.

She splits her time between the Pacific Northwest in the summer, and more southerly, warmer climes in the winter.

For more information about Bonita, please visit **www.bonitabellandersen.com**.

For more information about this book and the topics it addresses, please visit **suddenlywealthy.net**.

Book a Chat with Bonita

Because you're on this page it's highly likely that you have read at least part of this book, *Suddenly Wealthy*. You may be looking for ways to transform your investing experience, learn more, or just get started, period.

Good call, because once you've made that decision, your whole experience around money could start changing.

You could possibly start enjoying more peace of mind, confidence and a sense of security, knowing that with asking the right questions, you have a better chance of getting meaningful answers!

My goal is to help you with that, but because I don't know you, I can't say for sure.

And you probably don't know me that well either.

So, let's meet on Zoom or on a phone call, get to know each other, and figure this thing out.

If we determine that we need to discuss things further, we can talk about the different ways I work with clients. Of course, you'll be able to ask me questions as well.

The only thing I ask is that you come to the initial online meeting seriously committed to looking at benchmarking your financial freedom goals and implementing the findings into your life, if they make sense, and we both agree that it's a good idea for you.

I only work with a limited number of athletes at a time, so if now is not the right time to be looking at creating this plan, then lets determine that and feel free to bookmark this page to come back to when the time is right for you.

If you think this would be helpful to you, then please go ahead and book a time for us to chat. I look forward to meeting you.

You have my heartfelt wishes for all the best life has to offer, an amazing athletic career, and then an amazing life after sports. As with anything else in life, being prepared goes a long way toward reaching your goals. Thank you for allowing me to help you in this very important personal matter. I look forward to hearing from you—again, if you have any questions about the topics covered in this book, go to **https://bonitabellandersen.com/contact/**.

Happy reading!

To schedule an appointment:
https://calendly.com/bonita-8/60min?month

End Notes

1   https://en.wikipedia.org/wiki/Synchronicity
2   https://robincolucci.com/
3   https://dehoco.com/team
4   https://www.starwars.com/news/the-starwars-com-10-best-yoda-quotes
5   Jeanne Sahadi, "7 Traits the Rich Have in Common," CNN Money, June
    2, 2014, http://money.cnn.com/2014/06/01/luxury/rich-personality-
    traits/index.html
6   "The Pursuit of Happiness, accessed August 16, 2020, https://www.pursuit-
    of-happiness.org/science-of-happiness/how-to-be-happy-quick-tips/
7   FantasyPros Staff, "Who had the Most Accurate NFL Mock Draft in
    2020?" FantasyPros.com, April 27, 2020, -in-2020/
8   John Rampton, "Twenty Signs You're Destined to be a Millionaire,"
    Entrepreneur, accessed August 16, 2020, https://www.entrepreneur.com/
    slideshow/306791
9   "Odds of a High School Athlete Playing Pro Sports," Scholarshipstats.
    com, accessed August 16, 2020, http://www.scholarshipstats.com/odds-
    of-going-pro.htm
10 "Estimated Probability of Competing in Professional Sports," NCAA.
    org, April 8, 2020, http://www.ncaa.org/about/resources/research/
    estimated-probability-competing-professional-athletics

11 "Why Do Lottery Winners Go Broke?" Snow Financial Group, accessed August 11, 2020, https://snowgroupllc.com/blog/why-do-lottery-winners-go-broke

12 Tim Parker, "Why Athletes Go Broke," Investopedia, last modified May 31,2020, https://www.investopedia.com/financial-edge/0312/why-athletes-go-broke.aspx

13 Dr. Brad Klontz, "Money Disorder Assessment," https://www.yourmentalwealth.com/assessment/

14 Acronyms and Slang, http://acronymsandslang.com/meaning-of/chat-and-sub-cultures/NFL.html

15 "Highest-paid NFL players in 2020, ranked," CBS News, accessed August 12, 2020, https://www.cbsnews.com/pictures/highest-paid-nfl-players-who-has-the-top-salary-in-2020/

16 Noel King, "Young, Famous and Newly Rich: A Family Dilemma for Pro Athletes," Marketplace, May 23, 2013, https://www.marketplace.org/2013/05/23/young-famous-and-newly-rich-family-dilemma-pro-athletes/

17 Alicia Hemingway, "When Athletes Get Divorced: Sports Stars' Splits are Pricey," Divorce Saloon International, June 16, 2017, http://www.divorcesaloon.com/2017/06/16/when-athletes-gets-divorced/

18 Russ Alan Prince, "How to Avoid Financial Predators," Forbes, October 30, 2017, https://www.forbes.com/sites/russalanprince/2017/10/30/how-to-avoid-financial-predators/#231cbd1ee5ef

19 Lynette Gil, "8 of the Worst Financial Blunders by Athletes," Think Advisor, December 18, 2017, https://www.thinkadvisor.com/2017/12/18/8-of-the-worst-financial-blunders-by-athletes/

20 Stephanie Loiacono, "Rules That Warren Buffet Lives By," Investopedia, updated Jun 30, 2019, https://www.investopedia.com/financial-edge/0210/rules-that-warren-buffett-lives-by.aspx

21 Kim Kiyosaki, "What is Financial Freedom?" Rich Dad, updated April 4, 2019, https://www.richdad.com/what-is-financial-freedom

22 "How Most Millionaires Got Rich," Business News Daily, https://www.businessnewsdaily.com/2871-how-most-millionaires-got-rich.html

23 Thomas J. Stanley and William D. Danko, *The Millionaire Next Door: The Surprising Secrets of America's Wealthy*, (Longstreet Press: 1996)

24 Ilana Polyak, "Sudden wealth can leave you broke," CNBC, October 1, 2014, https://www.cnbc.com/2014/10/01/sudden-wealth-can-leave-you-broke.html

25 John, ESI Money, "I asked 100 millionaires how they spend, save, and invest, and they told me exactly what I expected to hear," Business Insider, December 5, 2018, https://www.businessinsider.com/how-millionaires-manage-money-interviews-2018-12

26 Vincent Frank, "Russell Wilson Contract: Seahawks QB Becomes NFL's Highest-Paid Player," Forbes, April 16, 2019, https://www.forbes.com/sites/vincentfrank/2019/04/16/russell-wilson-contract-seahawks-qb-becomes-nfls-highest-paid-player/#701636e34873

27 SI Wire, "What is Tom Brady's Net Worth?" SI NFL, February 5, 2017, https://www.si.com/nfl/2017/02/05/tom-brady-net-worth

28 Caitlyn Holroyd, "Federer Tops Forbes' 2020 List of Highest-paid Athletes," The Score, accessed August 13, 2020, https://www.thescore.com/atp/news/1975738

29 From November 2017 interview with Olympian Lauryn Williams

30 2017 Interview at the Sports Financial Advisor Conference, Scottsdale, AZ

31 J.D. Roth, "Learning to Use Money as a Tool," Get Rich Slowly, January 22, 2010, https://www.getrichslowly.org/learning-to-use-money-as-a-tool/

32 Tom Corley, "There are 4 Main Paths to Becoming a Millionaire—And This is the Easiest One, says Money Expert," CNBC, September 27, 2019, https://www.cnbc.com/2019/09/27/4-main-paths-to-becoming-millionaire-here-is-the-easiest-way-says-money-expert.html

33 Mark Stock, "Pro Athletes, Pay Cuts, and the COVID-19 Pandemic," The Manual, May 4, 2020, https://www.themanual.com/culture/pay-cuts-for-athletes-covid-19-pandemic/

34 Brett Rudy, "Defining the Difference Between Average and Median Salary," Salary.com, June 5, 2019, https://www.salary.com/blog/defining-the-difference-between-average-and-median-salary/

35 Kevin Draper, "Major League Soccer Reaches a Deal with Its Players," New York Times, February 6, 2020, https://www.nytimes.com/2020/02/06/sports/soccer/major-league-soccer-reaches-a-deal-with-its-players.html

36 Jim Woodruff, "How Much Money Does an NFL Player Make a Year?" Chron, Updated July 1, 2018, https://work.chron.com/much-money-nfl-player-make-year-2377.html

37 Average player salary in Major League Baseball from 2003 to 2020, Statista.com, Accessed August 14, 2020, https://www.statista.com/statistics/236213/mean-salaray-of-players-in-majpr-league-baseball/

38 Tom Huddleston Jr., "These are the highest paid players in the NBA right now," CNBC Make It, updated October 22, 2019, https://www.cnbc.com/2019/10/22/highest-paid-players-in-the-nba-right-now.html

39 Chris Martin, "Is There a Gender Pay Gap in Sports?" Payscale.com, May 21, 2018, https://www.payscale.com/data/gender-pay-gap-sports

40 SheIS Collective, https://www.sheissport.com/

41 Selena Hill, "Top WNBA Salaries Vs. NBA Salaries," Black Enterprise.com, April 12, 2019, https://www.blackenterprise.com/top-wnba-nba-salaries-2019/

42 David Berri, "Why Is the Michael Jordan of the WNBA Paid Less Than Adonis Jordan In 1999?" Forbes, July 9, 2018, https://www.forbes.com/sites/davidberri/2018/07/09/why-isnt-the-michael-jordan-of-the-wnba-paid-at-least-as-well-as-adonis-jordan-was/#15d18576dce5

43 Jenn Hatfield, "WNBA attendance declines in 2018: What does that mean for the league?" Medium, August 29, 2018, https://medium.com/her-hoop-stats/wnba-attendance-declines-in-2018-what-does-that-mean-for-the-league-4b88e59583f1

44 Associated Press, "Some WNBA teams downsizing arenas to help bottom line," USA Today, July 9, 2018, https://www.usatoday.com/story/sports/wnba/2018/07/09/some-wnba-teams-downsizing-arenas-to-help-bottom-line/36737011/

45 https://blog.barrystickets.com/nba-ticket-prices/#:~:text=The%20average%20NBA%20ticket%20price, prices%20on%20the%20secondary%20market

46 https://www.statista.com/statistics/193714/regular-season-home-attendance-of-national-basketball-association-teams-in-2010/

47 Jim Woodruff, "Salary Range for Women Pro Golfers," Chron.com, August 27, 2018, https://work.chron.com/salary-range-women-pro-golfers-2627.html

48 https://www.shmoop.com/careers/gymnast/salary.html#:~:text=Expected%20Lifetime%20Earnings %3A%20%241% 2C252%2C440, the%20millions%20if%20you%20win

49 "National Women's Hockey League," Wikipedia, https://en.wikipedia.org/wiki/National_Women%27s_Hockey_League

50 Anne M. Peterson and The Associated Press, "USWNT Paid More Than the Men Over Past Eight Years, U.S. Soccer Says," Denver Post, July 29, 2019, https://www.denverpost.com/2019/07/29/us-women-soccer-paid-more-than-men/

51 https://www.cbc.ca/sports/tennis/naomi-osaka-worlds-highest-paid-female-athlete-1.5580667

52 https://www.sportscasting.com/the-top-10-highest-paid-female-athletes-are-all-tennis-players/

53 "Highest Paid WWE Divas 2020," Sportekz.com, December 10, 2019, https://www.sportekz.com/list/highest-paid-wwe-divas/

54 Garrett Parker, "Here's The 20 Richest WWE Divas Of All-Time," Money Inc., accessed August 16, 2020, https://moneyinc.com/the-20-richest-wwe-divas-of-all-time/

55 Oliver Browning, "WWE Salaries for 2019 Show a Massive Pay Gap Between Male and Female Superstars," GiveMeSport.com, November 01, 2019, https://www.givemesport.com/1537045-wwe-salaries-for-2019-show-a-massive-pay-gap-between-male-and-female-superstars

56 Anne Gaviola, "Why It's So Easy for Pro Athletes to Blow Their Millions," Vice, September 17, 2019, https://www.vice.com/en_ca/article/wjwxmq/why-its-so-easy-for-pro-athletes-to-blow-their-millions

57 Bianca Miller Cole, "2 Reasons Women Are Truly Better With Money—In Business and Personal Lives," Forbes, June 19, 2019, https://www.forbes.com/sites/biancamillercole/2019/06/19/are-women-truly-better-with-money/#11a497db71af

58 Jessica Walrack, "The Scientific Reason Why Money Makes Us Happy," SuperMoney, January 18, 2020, https://www.supermoney.com/money-happy/

59 Robin Goist, "LeBron James Family Foundation to renovate Akron apartment building into transitional housing for I Promise School students and families," Cleveland.com, November 4, 2019, i-promise-school-students-and-families.html

60 "Antoine Walker Explains How He Lost $110 Million," YouTube, October https://www.youtube.com/watch?v=oNaw2bk39jY

61 Marguerite Ward, "NBA star reveals what he learned from losing $100 million and going bankrupt," CNBC Make It, July 8, 2016, https://www.cnbc.com/2016/07/08/nba-star-antoine-walker-reveals-what-he-learned-from-losing-100-million.html#:~:text=Over%20his%2012%2Dyear%20career,7%20bankruptcy%20in%20May%202010.

62 Jane Wollman Rusoff, "Ex-NBA Star Says He Should've Listened to His Financial Advisor," Think Advisor, June 28, 2019, https://www.thinkadvisor.com/2019/06/28/ex-nba-star-says-he-shouldve-listened-to-his-financial-advisor/

63 "How to Win the Money Game: A Former NBA Star Shares Financial Advice," NPR, June 27, 2015, http://www.npr.org/2015/06/27/416793011/former-nba-star-explains-how-to-win-the-money-game

64 Scott Davis, "Former NBA Player Who's Written About Managing Finances Shares What Draft Prospects Should Know About Handling Life in The League," Business Insider, June 22, 2017, http://www.businessinsider.com/adonal-foyle-financial-advice-nba-draft-prospects-2017-6

65 Adonal Foyle, *Winning the Money Game: Lessons Learned from the Financial Fouls of Athletes*, (HarperCollins, 2015)

66 Garrett Parker, "20 Retired Pro Athletes Who Now Work Normal Jobs," Money Inc., accessed August 16, 2020, https://moneyinc.com/20-retired-pro-athletes-who-now-work-normal-jobs/

67 NFLPA Externship, NFLPA, https://nflpa.com/active-players/externships

68 Chris Roling, "10 Current Athletes Who Are Ridiculously Charitable," Bleacher Report, August 8, 2016, https://bleacherreport.com/articles/2656316-10-current-athletes-who-are-ridiculously-charitable

69 LeBron James profile, Forbes, https://www.forbes.com/profile/lebron-james/

70 https://www.maryanneradmacher.net/

71 Terrance Ross, "10 Pro Athletes Who Ended Up In the Poorhouse," Men's Journal, accessed August 16, 2020, https://www.mensjournal.com/sports/10-pro-athletes-who-ended-up-in-the-poor-house/

72 Nicole Shepard, "Most American High Schoolers Don't Know How to Manage Money," Deseret.com, July 24, 2014, https://www.deseret.com/2014/7/24/20545131/most-american-high-schoolers-don-t-know-how-to-manage-money

73 Debra Adams Simmons, "Lebron's Love For Akron Shows Promises Kept, Lives He's Changed," The Undefeated.com, June 21, 2016, Https://Theundefeated.Com/Features/Lebrons-Love-For-Akron-Shows-Promises-Kept-Lives-Hes-Changed/

74 Kelli Pate, "Patriots Player Rob Gronkowski is Retiring from the NFL with $54 Million of His Career Earnings. Here Are 5 Money-Saving Tips You Can Learn From Him," Business Insider, March 25, 2019, https://www.businessinsider.com/nfl-patriots-money-saving-tips-rob-gronkowski-2019-2

75 Maurie Backman, "The Reason 37% of Families Are Forced to Rely on Credit Cards," The Ascent, February 23, 2020, ool.com/the-ascent/credit-cards/articles/reason-families-are-forced-rely-credit-cards/

76 Leigh Steinberg, "5 Reasons Why 80% of Retired NFL Players Go Broke," Forbes, February, 9, 2015, https://www.forbes.com/sites/leighsteinberg/2015/02/09/5-reasons-why-80-of-retired-nfl-players-go-broke/#4470718478cc

77 Associated Press, "Former Starts Explain Why NFL Players Go Broke, and What You Can Learn From Them," Business Insider, October 10, 2017, https://www.businessinsider.com/ap-liz-weston-why-nfl-players-go-broke-and-what-you-can-learn-2017-10

78 Rodney Brooks, "Why Do So Many Pros Go Broke?" The Undefeated.com, March 24, 2017, https://theundefeated.com/features/why-do-so-many-pros-go-broke/

79 Peter Socotch, "Here's What Russell Wilson Bought His Offensive Line for Christmas," Yahoo Sports, December 25, 2019, https://sports.yahoo.com/heres-russell-wilson-bought-offensive-175634552.html

80 "Brady Takes Care of His OL... Buys Them 42K Cars," PatsFans.com forum, https://www.patsfans.com/new-england-patriots/messageboard/threads/brady-takes-care-of-his-ol-buys-them-42k-cars-merged.82881/

81 Tim Parker, "6 Rules From 6 of the World's Top Investors," Investopedia, February 1, 2020, https://www.investopedia.com/articles/financial-theory/11/6-lessons-top-6-investors.asp

82 https://www.putnam.com/literature/pdf/II508.pdf

83 Mark J. Perry, "More Evidence That It's Very Hard to 'Beat the Market' Over Time, 95% of Finance Professionals Can't Do It," AEI.org, March

20, 2018, https://www.aei.org/carpe-diem/more-evidence-that-its-very-hard-to-beat-the-market-over-time-95-of-financial-professionals-cant-do-it/

84 Jack Dougherty, "Are NFL Mock Drafts Ever Accurate or Should You Just Ignore Them?" Sportscasting.com, April 15, 2020, https://www.sportscasting.com/are-nfl-mock-drafts-ever-accurate-or-should-you-just-ignore-them/

85 Pete Pachal, "How Kodak Squandered Every Single Digital Opportunity It Had," Mashable.com, January 20, 2012, https://mashable.com/2012/01/20/kodak-digital-missteps/

86 Stacy Rapacon, "How Often Do Stock Market Corrections Happen?" Grow.Acorns.com, February 13, 2018, https://grow.acorns.com/how-often-do-stock-market-corrections-happen/

87 Andrew Hallam, "Are Investors as Dumb as This Study Says?" AssetBuilder, April 11, 2019, https://assetbuilder.com/knowledge-center/articles/are-investors-as-dumb-as-this-study-says

88 Dana Anspach, "Why Average Investors Earn Below Average Market Returns,"The Balance.com, January 28, 2019, https://www.thebalance.com/why-average-investors-earn-below-average-market-returns-2388519

89 Time in the Market concept: https://www.putnam.com/literature/pdf/II508.pdf

90 James Chen, "Asset Allocation," Investopedia.com, April 26, 2020, https://www.investopedia.com/articles/investing/103013/stocks-remain-best-longterm-bet.asp

91 "Top 15 Reasons To Hire A Money Coach," FinancialMentor.com, https://financialmentor.com/financial-coaching/benefits/top-15-reasons-to-hire-a-money-coach

92 Bill Crager, Christian Berthelsen, "Ex-NBA Star Chuck Person, Advisors, Coaches Charged in NCAA Bribe Scam," Financial Advisor Magazine, September 26, 2017, https://www.fa-mag.com/news/ex-nba-star-chuck-person-among-coaches-charged-in-bribe-scam-34871.html

93 James Pollard, "7 Client Referral Ideas to Help You Get More Referrals," TheAdvisorCoach.com, accessed August 16, 2020, https://www.theadvisorcoach.com/7-client-referral-ideas-to-help-you-get-more-referrals.html

94 Stephen A. Schwartz, "Is Active Management Really Dead?" Worth.com, February 28, 2018, https://www.worth.com/advice/is-active-management-really-dead/

95 The Journal of Finance, Vol XLVII, No. 2, June 1992, "The Cross-Section of Expected Stock Returns", Eugene F. Fama and Kenneth R French

96 "Firms Claiming Compliance with the GIPS Standards," GIPSStandards.com, accessed August 16, 2020, https://www.gipsstandards.org/compliance/Pages/firms_claiming_compliance.aspx

[97] "Number of Investment Companies Reporting to Investment Company Institute in the United States from 1997 to 2019," Statista.com, accessed August 16, 2020, https://www.statista.com/statistics/295692/investment-companies-number-united-states/

[98] Megan Leonhardt, "Budgets are 'pointless,' one financial coach says—here's what to do with your money instead," CNBC Make It, May 6, 2019, https://www.cnbc.com/2019/05/06/ramit-sethi-budgets-are-pointless-heres-what-to-do-instead.html

[99] Stein, David, "Are You Investing, Speculating or Gambling?" last modified November 30, 2020, https://moneyfortherestofus.com/mny143-investing-speculating-gambling/

www.ingramcontent.com/pod-product-compliance
Lightning Source LLC
Chambersburg PA
CBHW070932210326
41520CB00021B/6915